I Attest and Affirm
Speaking Life & Empowerment for Women by Women

Amalia Lewis
Ayeisha Latta-Matthews
Carol Terrell
Jade Cross-French
Ke'sha Dennis
Maureen Michelle Brewster
Serita Love
Twanda Grey, LCSW

**MAWMedia Group
Reno NV**

Publisher: MAWMedia Group

© 2020 Twanda Grey

All rights reserved. This book or any portion thereof may not be reproduced or used in any manner whatsoever without the express written permission of the publisher except for the use of brief quotations in a book review or scholarly journal.

Second Edition: February 2020

I Attest and Affirm: Speaking Life & Empowerment for Women by Women/ By Amalia Lewis, Ayeisha Latta-Matthews, Carol Terrell, Jade Cross-French, Ke'sha Dennis, Maureen Michelle Brewster, Serita Love, Twanda Grey

ISBN: 978-1-943616-25-1

MAWMedia Group, LLC
3095 Fairwood Dr
Reno, NV 89502

www.mawmedia.com

Biographies

Serita Love is an Englewood native from Chicago, a mom and self-professed "Success Junkie" who educates by combining BOOK and STREET smarts. As the founder of the Personal and Professional Achievement brand Success Junkie™, she provides tools and resources that inspire excellence. She is a Relational, Group, and Organizational professional who has a background that includes: Community Outreach, Public Speaking, Special Events and Integrated Marketing Communications. She has worked on countless experiential marketing and guerrilla marketing campaigns for many Fortune 500 Brands such as: Starbuck's, P&G, & Safeway, Inc. She is also a proud Rotarian, woman of Alpha Kappa Alpha Sorority, and a Spokesperson for the Urban Intellectuals brand.

While working specifically with the youth and women to attain their personal and professional goals, Serita consistently produces an innovative approach to every new opportunity placed before her. She pushes people beyond their own personal barriers, so they can get out into the world and become the person they deserve to be. By implementing personal branding, marketing and goal setting strategies, she ensures people success at the level of their effort and commitment.

Serita has produced and has participated in countless conferences, seminars, workshops and panel discussions. In her spare time, she enjoys volunteering, reading about business and leadership, traveling, roller skating and spending time with her son, Anius (A-ny-us). Her motto: "It's okay to get hooked on ambition."

 **Amalia Lewis** was born in Houston, Texas and raised in Hampton Virginia. She is an active duty military member that has serving more than 17 years in the United States Air Force. She obtained her Bachelorette Degree in Healthcare Administration from Purdue University, and is pursuing her master's degree in Human Service's Counseling. She currently works in an Operational Medicine facility, which provides medical care for 3,000 active duty military members. She is a single mother of two beautiful girls, Adriana Ginae 14, and Alexandra Jade, 4.

Ke'sha Dennis is a serial entrepreneur with a passion for financial literacy and wealth building. From her early experiences in Oakland, California Ke'sha developed a keen understanding of the challenges facing families and women in particular. Influenced by care of her grandmother, she began her college education in search of a nursing degree. She discovered a more specific calling in leadership and entrepreneurship.

After some success in the corporate world, Ke'sha became a tax preparer and found her way into the financial arena with the realization of the immense impact finances play on health and well-being. With that foundation, she has continued to develop her ventures into multiple areas of women's empowerment including entrepreneurship, life coaching, financial coaching and spirituality. Ke'sha believes that self-development is the key to health and well-being. You can change if you establish the vision and put in the work. She is living proof of your ability to transform.

Her latest endeavor is Lady Buzz Conversations That Create Movement, a non-profit that has a Facebook community with over 4000 members. She sponsors the group to promote conversations that create movement having noticed that Black women needed a space to exchange their expertise and network with other influencers. The site is active with dozens of posts per day.

http://www.upscaletaxprofessionals.com
http://www.ladybuzz.org

 **Twanda Grey** currently resides in Connecticut with her husband of 27 years. She has two adult sons, an adult stepdaughter who is married and two beautiful grandchildren.

She currently own/operate her own business, Strategic Resolutions LLC (SR) which is a human service consultant agency providing services in many capacities to empower individuals in "Building A Better YOU!".

She is also a Licensed Psychotherapist and operates a clinical practice under the Hub of SR serving individuals in need of emotional and mental health services.

She is a College Professor teaching in the discipline of Social Work, Sociology and Early Childhood Education. Twanda is an author and recently published the book "Authentically You." She is also a member of the first African American Greek Sorority-Alpha Kappa Alpha Sorority Inc and a member of the National Coalition of 100 Black Women Inc in which both organizations strive to advocate on behalf of Black women and girls to promote leadership development and gender equity in the areas of health, education and economic empowerment.

For more information visit Twanda Grey at www.twandagrey.org and/or www.strategicresolutionsct.com.

 **Carol Terrell** is the Founder and CEO of Onyx Capital Enterprise. She is a Singmopreneur, Evangelist, and Financial Coach whom operates a Financial Resource Hub where we create Wealth with Options! I am a mother of 3 phenomenal daughters and the grandmother of 3 handsome grandsons. I create goals, strategies, objectives, and tactics to ensure you obtain education, stability, credit worthiness, and financial freedom. My goal is to educate and empower our community, and the world on how to be a better steward over their finances. Through my company I offer financial education, coaching, and accountability. In addition, I offer credit restoration services, credit report education, and credit repair training to help you understand your credit report and the importance of keeping it clean and accurate. I am very passionate about financial coaching because this is something very close to my heart. I have firsthand experience because I have already traveled the road of messed of credit, lack of financial education, and brokenness. I pride myself on helping my clients change their mindset and behavior around finances, offering client support along their journey. I care about the work that I produce, and it's important that my clients are satisfied and elated about their financial future. I love getting my clients excited about the journey, and the doors that will open to **Credit Worthiness, Financial Freedom, and Multiple Streams of Income.** Let's get started on your journey to **Change, Educate, Discipline, Empower, and Maintain** to Become The Master Of Your Destiny! Contact me at www.onyxcapitalenterise.com at carol@carolterrell.com or Instagram @onyx_capital_enterprise.

**Jade Cross-French.** Jade Cross-French is the founder and CEO of Young Gifted Hustler and CrossFrench Financials. Motivated by her community and family, she has been an outstanding asset to many influencers, organizations, and businesses throughout Chicago.

Jade has a strong desire to bring prosperity back into the households nationwide. Jade is extremely innovative and has a lot to contribute, and she loves dialogue. Even when conversations get tough, it is not in her nature to shy away from those conversations.

Jade has been known to share the success stories of young entrepreneurs who beat the odds just like her. She educates young people on the skills she wished she possess during the transition from high school to adulthood. She thrives to educate families to build wealth. Jade is a lifelong student and enjoys experiencing real world socioeconomics. Her main goal is to help transform the lives she comes across. Jade is a go getter and she have a track record to prove it.

Ayeisha L. Latta-Matthews. Ayeisha is originally from Queens, New York. She is a 20-year Air Force veteran. She obtained her Bachelor of Science in Criminal Justice (2010) and is currently pursuing her Master of Science (M.S.) in Counseling with a specialization in Clinical Mental Health Counseling (CMHC). Currently, she is enjoying retired life, while continuing to be an anointed evangelist, mompreneur, philanthropist, motivational speaker, prayer warrior, and visionista. She is a fiancé and mother of two beautiful daughters, Myeisha, 15 and Rhianna, 12.

Maureen Michelle Brewster. Maureen Michelle Brewster is a native-born New Yorker, she has served over 25 years in federal service with the U.S. Army and U.S. Postal Service. She is an Author and Business Consultant. She holds two Master's Degrees, one in Human Resource Management and the other in Performance Improvement. She is currently pursuing her Doctorate in Human Resource Management and Organizational Behavior. Currently, she resides in the state of Florida.

Maureen Michelle Brewster is the CEO of M.Brewster & Associates, whose focus is on small businesses, entrepreneurs and nonprofits. By providing consultancy direction in the areas of business plans, proposals, strategic marketing, human resource management, and analytical data research. Maureen is also an independent travel agency owner. MB Travels believes in making business and travel synonymous with "living your best life" while ensuring all work equals more leisure time.

Contents

- **Biographies** 5
- **Section I: Attitudes** 18
- **Forgiveness** 19
- **Peace** 21
- **Authenticity** 23
- **Judgment** 26
- **Understanding** 28
- **Birthing** 31
- **Encouragement** 33
- **Faith** 35
- **Hope** 38
- **Peace** 40
- **Grace** 43
- **Patience** 45
- **Healing** 47
- **Expectations** 50
- **Gratitude** 52
- **Jealousy** 55
- **Comfort** 57
- **Wisdom** 59
- **Transformed** 62
- **Miracles** 64
- **Karma** 67

Strength	69
Calling	71
Anger	73
Positivity	75
Loyalty	78
Vision	80
Discipline	82
Goodness	85
Learning	87
Joy	90
Genuineness	92
Love	94
Praise	96
Friendship	99
Light	102
Service	104
Forward	106
Success	108
Love	111
Abundance	113
Agreement	115
Saints and Sinners	117
Sinner & Saint	119
God's Plan	121
I Am No Longer Broken	123
I Am Encouraged	126
What to do with Your Life	128

Embracing His Will	131
Your Inner Light	133
Embrace Your Calling	135
Shameless I am	138
I Am Bold	140
God Answers	142
Despair is Temporary	144
Live in the Present	147
I Am Better	149
I Will Break Generational Curses	151
The Gift of Praise	153
Loving God	156
It Wasn't My Fault	158
Start Trusting	160
I Speak Wealth, Abundance and Life	162
Speak Wisely	165
Speak Life	167
Choose Your Words Wisely	169
Yes HE Can	171
I Am Secure	174
Suicide Loses	176
I Have Friends That Understand	178
I Am Alive	180
I Will Guard My Surroundings	182
Through the Eyes of Depression	185
I Will Not Argue	187
I Trust You	189

I Will Wait on the Lord 192
I Receive My Healing 194
I Will Listen to the Lord 197
Aim for a Forgiving Heart 199

Section I: Attitudes

Forgiveness

Matthew 6: 14-15

> For if you forgive other people when they sin against you, your heavenly Father will also forgive you. But if you do not forgive others their sins, your Father will not forgive your sins.

I attest and affirm...

When it is all said and done, the most important thing you can do is forgive. We will be disappointed more times than we can even count. We will have expectations that we shouldn't have for people and they will let us down. You will be accused for wrongdoing that isn't even in alignment with what you value and who you are. Accept that apology that you will never receive. I know that sounds odd, but it's just something you must do. When you forgive those, who haven't asked for forgiveness, you find an inner peace like no other.

Forgiveness is a gift that you give yourself. It is powerful, because it is peaceful. Those who have not asked for forgiveness, may have pride, confusions and other demons to face. It is not your responsibility to dwell on the things you cannot change. You can't change other people's moods, behaviors, and attitudes. Don't even bother to try.

I've had to forgive countless times in my life. It is never a surprise to me that I am relieved after doing so. I believe that when you don't forgive, you grant people permission to live in your mind rent free. This is toxic. It will leave you unproductive.

God sees us in our best and worse. Yet, we are still forgiven. Keep that in mind when you are faced with challenging situations that frustrates you to the point that you become cold inside. Forgive them like God forgives you and move on. Forgiveness provides you with a level of inner peace that is rewarding. You'll thank yourself later.

Serita Love

Peace

Philippians 4:7

And the peace of God which passes all understanding shall keep your hearts and minds through Christ Jesus.

I attest and affirm...

From this day forward, I am living my best life. I am living in the peace of God which passes all understanding. There is peace, and then there is the peace of God which keeps your hearts and minds through Christ Jesus. When I finally let go and let God my life started changing for the better. I began to experience life more abundantly, meaning I had ammunition, and I was afforded a special kind of tool to add to my toolbox. The name of that tool is PEACE. When you get to a place when you are sick and tired of being sick and tired, YOU WILL speak the words ENOUGH IS ENOUGH. When you get to this point your peace has been compromised, your happiness has been shattered, and your joy has turned to sadness.

Let me give you a word of advice. The world nor people have given you peace, happiness, or joy. So, why are you allowing them to take those things from you? Only God gives you peace, happiness, and joy. He does not remove those things from you. When you no longer have peace, you compromise your happiness, and you destroy your joy. The devil comes to steal, kill, and destroy. The only way he can do that is when your foundation and your grounding (The Word of God) is shaken. You are being tried and put to the test. God gave permission to the devil to try Job. He asked Satan about his good and faithful servant Job. God told Satan he could not kill Job. I want you to know that Satan must ask God for permission to try you.

We all have areas of vulnerabilities. They are called weaknesses because those areas are the areas that our foundation is fragile, with openings and cracks which allow Satan is to creep into our hearts and minds to remind us of our shortcomings. He will use them against us, day in and day out. What he is doing here is manipulating our minds, creating a place of uncertainty in our minds, making us question who we are, pulling us further away from God's perfect peace. God's perfect peace is an inner peace that resides in your bone marrow. It marinates in your soul, and it is tender to your hearts. I attest and affirm that your will no longer reside in darkness. You will walk boldly out of the wilderness. God's perfect peace, that peace that surpasses all understanding, will abide in you forever.

Carol Terrell

Authenticity

Psalm 139:14

I am fearfully and wonderfully made.

I attest and affirm...

I will celebrate my worth. It is so easy to feel defeated at points in our lives during trials and tribulations. And during these times, instead of challenging ourselves to process the root issues, we ignore them and mask the issues. This can happen so much that we end up having several masks hanging on the wall that we wear interchangeably just to keep up with the facade.

Perhaps the most binding thing about the masks we wear is the fact that some of those masks were hand created by our guardians and caretakers from birth and delicately handed to us. We are molded by a compilation of people, events, and experiences. We rarely take inventory to assess if the values and beliefs bestowed upon us previously are what we value and believe today.

Introducing the creation of the "Mask." Masking emotions like hurt; defeat; fear; inadequate; failure- and we pretend. We wear the mask that covers such emotions and pretend to be. Masks feel safe but they are dangerous because these "created" masks create false truths about ourselves so much that we actually begin to believe; and we become great at hiding the authenticity of who we REALLY are.

We live in a society that thrives on labels. A person's race, sexuality, socioeconomic status, and titles name several. Labels give people a sense of order. And for some people, the desires to belong and fit in can leave one questioning "Who am I?" versus affirming "I know who I am!"

We are too dynamic to be placed in a box and labeled because labels never adequately capture the complexity of the human spirit.

Getting to the core of "who we are" entails ridding ourselves of the mask, tossing the assigned labels, and aborting the perception of what we "think" we know about ourselves. It entails embracing the unquestionable YOU and being vulnerable enough to say with conviction, "This is who I am flaws and all. I am fearfully and wonderfully made." It entails walking boldly in that statement and owning it as truth.

Give yourself permission to show up in your own life! Free yourself from what others have conditioned you to be so that you can embrace the person you are meant to be. Challenge yourself to no longer merely exist but to Live life Authentically. What are you waiting for? The time is "NOW!"

Twanda Grey

Psalm 139:14

I am fearfully and wonderfully made.

I attest and affirm....

_____
_____
_____
_____
_____
_____
_____
_____
_____
_____
_____
_____
_____
_____
_____
_____
_____
_____
_____

Judgment

Luke 6:37 (ESV)

Judge not, and you will not be judged; condemn not, and you will not be condemned; forgive, and you will be forgiven.

I attest and affirm...

I will love my brother and sister and approach each situation with objectivity. I will not judge what I do not know. I will love those around me. I will forgive those just as I would like to be forgiven. I am not perfect; however, I serve a perfect God who loves me and sent his only begotten son to die for my sins.

I will not speak ill of others. I will speak life into them, just as I would like for people to speak life into me. When people around me are down, I will do my best to assist them in whatever manner I am able. If it is just a word, I will seek through prayer to give them that word.

When others need assistance, I will not judge the person or the situation. Neither of them is mine to judge. I will proceed with an open mind, and a loving heart. The words that I speak will be kind. The help I give will be genuine. I am a child of God, and I want all who enter my presence to see Him. He is the way, the truth, and the life.

When people come to speak to me, I will listen and not judge. If I am given any advice, I will make sure that it is congruent with your instruction so that I am not led astray. Every lesson needed to learn is written in your holy word with complete instructions.

If I have a hard time not passing judgment, I will take it to you in prayer and seek your guidance. My heart will maintain its complement of love. I will gain knowledge and understanding resulting in a less judgmental space and a more loving space.

Amalia Lewis

Understanding

Proverbs 19:8

> The one who gets wisdom loves life; the one who cherishes understanding will soon prosper.

I attest and affirm...

I am wise, because I've chosen to be a student of life. Daily, I attempt to learn a new skill that will advance me to the next step. The ability to constantly open my mind to the new discoveries God has in store for me, is like living a dream. When I rise every morning, I'm excited to seek what God has in store for me. I have released the need to be in control, because God has my days planned. Understanding that God is in control, releases me from the chains of failure, fear, hurt, defeat and pain. On days I feel less motivated, I use those days as learning experiences and to create my own peace through prayer and self-care. The joy comes from each day knowing we have another opportunity to be excellent.

Today I, Ke'sha Dennis, attest and affirm that I am renewed in the spirit of helping, love, peace, joy, grace, salvation and change. My trials and tribulations were necessary to become the woman I am today. God showed me love on days, I didn't know how to love myself. There is an inner undeniable peace that comes from understanding and knowing the Lord. To have God is to have wisdom.

Ke'sha Dennis

Proverbs 19:8

The one who gets wisdom loves life; the one who cherishes understanding will soon prosper.

I attest and affirm….

Birthing

Hebrews 11: 1

> Faith is the substance of things hoped for, the evidence of things not seen.

I attest and affirm...

All dreams can come true if you have the courage to pursue them, and the faith in God to manifest them. Our God is omnipotent (able to do anything) and he is omnipresent (infinite, widespread, and not limited to time or space). I started doing credit repair 8 years ago just to clean up my own credit. After I completed my credit transformation, people started asking me to work on theirs. At the time, I looked at it as a hobby. I discovered I was good at doing it. It turned into a passion for me because I love encouraging and helping others. I started my credit repair business.

Over the years, I changed how I was doing things. I started incorporating more beneficial services to my clients. I started praying to God that I wanted to reach people around the world and help others become masters of their destinies. I wanted to speak at seminars and workshops empowering others. I started praying again asking God for divine connections. Over the last two years, he gave me a new business name and a new direction which would take the business to another level. He later sent me a woman as my client that would later become my Executive Assistant. Unknown to me, that woman was praying for divine connections and asking God to send me the midwives that would birth the vision.

On August 3, 2019, I was filling in for an originally scheduled speaker at an event. I did not know the host of the event, and I did not know any of the other speakers. The host made a social media post asking for recommendations for credit repair. I was tagged in the post not knowing it was to speak at the event. I reached out to the young lady to answer questions. She asked if I could speak at the event. To God be the Glory because if I did not stand on my faith, if I waivered in my determination, if I did not have patience, if I had not let God use my story, I would have aborted his mission to bring my passion to fruition. That day on Aug 3, I met the midwives that my now Executive Assistant had prayed for. Those divine connections are currently helping to birth my vision and my passion.

I attest and affirm that it is your time. It is your season. The midwives are on the way but without faith those things hoped for are dead. Test your faith, try your faith, and test your faith again to see if your faith stands strong enough in God that the substance of those things hoped for will soon be the evidence of those things not seen. I am a living testimony of my Faith being the substance of things hoped for and the evidence of things not seen 8 years later. God has you! I dare you to try him, to trust him, and to have faith in him! Glory Hallelujah!

Carol Terrell

Encouragement

Deuteronomy 1:38

Encourage him.

I attest and affirm...

God employs his people to encourage one another. He did not say to an angel, "Gabriel, my servant Joshua is about to lead my people into Canaan-go, encourage him. "God never works needless miracles; if his purposes can be accomplished by ordinary means, he will not use miraculous agency. Gabriel would not have been half so well fitted for the work. A brother's sympathy is more precious than an angel's embassy.

I attest and affirm that having someone who went through the same test of faith that I did when my three-old son died was a great comfort to me. My family members could not relate because we had never experienced a death of a child so young. No amount of comfort was available to me, no shoulder of comfort because no one knew what words to say or how to help ease my grief. So, I buried my grief along with my son and moved through life in a haze.

One day I woke with the realization that I needed help, not sure what kind, I just did not feel right. I found my bible and searched for a passage, a scripture to find my answers. The above passage helped me to seek outside help. The passage below put an exclamation point on what I needed to do.

"An angel is better at knowing our Father's bidding than man's temper. For an angel has never experienced the harshness of the wilderness as Moses had done." Having someone share their experience with you about their trial can create a sisterly or brotherly bond. There will be times in our lives when we will need help. It can come from someone who may be a stranger, do not refuse if possible; God does all by his design and not ours. Remember God loves you and will never forsake you.

Maureen Brewster

Faith

Hebrew 11:1

Now Faith is the assurance of things hoped for, and the evidence of things not seen.

I attest and affirm...

I will patiently wait for "IT" to come to pass.

Faith. It's a word we hear thrown around all the time. "Keep the faith." "Walking in faith." "Having faith." Often, we speak these words from our mouths while our actions and behaviors do not match. It is difficult sometimes to believe the word as we wait for the things, we hope for to come to pass; causing a person to feel frustrated, anxious and impatient.

Every situation in life requires deciding how we will respond. It is true that we may not have total control of the things that may come our way, but we TOTALLY have control as to how we respond. We can remain patient and keep believing Gods' promises, or we can allow the enemy's words to fill our minds, make us miserable and lead us astray.

Patience is described as having the capacity to accept or tolerate delay, trouble, or suffering without getting angry or upset. We have become too used to immediate results and instant gratification. Patience is invaluable to use as a coping skill. Sometimes waiting is best because it helps develop the character of God in us.

Patience doesn't mean passivity or resignation, but power. It is an emotionally freeing practice of waiting, watching, and knowing when to act.

Having faith patiently means waiting your turn, knowing your turn will come, while believing for good things to happen. Having Faith changes how we live our lives and is a motivator to keep moving in life.

Faith is leaning entirely on God with absolute confidence in His power, wisdom and goodness. Faith believes that God can do what would otherwise be impossible. Faith trust God for what it cannot yet see.

Choose to develop a mindset of faith; Believe that God's power is in you and that God is working in your life right now!

Twanda Grey

Hebrew 11:1

Now Faith is the assurance of things hoped for, and the evidence of things not seen.

I attest and affirm....

_____
_____
_____
_____
_____
_____
_____
_____
_____
_____
_____
_____
_____
_____
_____
_____
_____
_____
_____
_____
_____

Hope

Romans 12:12

Rejoice in hope, be patient in tribulation, be constant in prayer.

I attest and affirm...

It will happen, but it will take time." Hope is a feeling of expectation and desire for a certain thing to happen". We hope for things, we dream about things, we desire things and we expect things. Be anxious for nothing. Do not rush your birthing process. I know it is hard sometimes when you want something to happen right away or you are experiencing hardship, difficulty, trauma, setback, or misfortune. Count it all joy when you are facing trials of many kinds and find yourselves swimming in the rough waters of tribulations. You are not to complain but rejoice in your hopes, dreams and expectations. Practice patience through the storms and submit your requests and burdens to God in constant prayer and supplication.

Do you know that you are resilient, and unbreakable? God hand molded each one of us knowing our strengths, and our weaknesses. He never will give us more then we can handle. We put more pressure on ourselves than God does. When we are struggling, we become faint, weak, sad, depressed, lonely, disappointed and let down however those are not things God placed on our cross. We added all those extra weights to our cross. We all have a cross to carry just like Jesus did when he carried our sins. The same process Jesus went through we too shall go through.

We are born, we are tested, we are broken in our tribulations where we die, meaning all the old has died and you are putting on the new (rebirth). We are like clay, and God molds us and then we go through this thing called life which breaks us down. God then comes back and remolds us to this new being. Just imagine yourself walking in Jesus shoes. The torture to his flesh, the spitting, the pain, the agony, the nails pierced into his body, and the crown of thorns pierced into his head. When our patience is short and we are no longer rejoicing in hope, being patient in tribulation or constant in prayer remind yourself of Jesus on that cross not complaining, the long suffering he endured when he gave up his last breath, the Holy Ghost to give us Salvation Everlasting.

Carol Terrell

Peace

Romans 14:19

> So then let us pursue what makes for peace and for mutual upbuilding.

I attest and affirm...

You will be peaceful in times of chaos. It takes a special level of strength to be peaceful at times when adverse conditions seem to override everything good happening in your life.

I remember having to find peace within myself during a dark time in my life. I wanted to be angry. I wanted to be evil. I got out of character, because I was hurt and disappointed. I hadn't felt so hurt in a long time, but I knew that I would have to find peace within, or I would take my anger and frustration out on others. Or worse, I would have lost my mind. I have no one but God to thank for allowing me to be still as I pressed "reset" on my state of being. You don't just wake up and feel better about things that could have broken you into pieces.

Discovering inner peace isn't always easy, but don't fret. You will put your faith in God to restore you. You will work diligently to figure things out and overcome the challenges you are or will be faced with. I firmly believe we are faced with certain challenges, because we can handle them. We just do not realize it at the time. However, when we pass the test of time, something incredible happens! Something comes over us. We become calm and peaceful. We get quiet and sometimes we isolate for a brief period; and this is healthy.

I pray that you have a healthy heart, mind and spirit as you find peace with yourself. Far too many seek peace in places that do not serve them. God already has a table set for you. You just must show up and let go of whatever it is that anchors you. Peace will afford you the opportunity to grow in ways you cannot even fathom. You deserve that, so get it! It's waiting got you.

Serita Love

Romans 14:19

So then let us pursue what makes for peace and for mutual upbuilding.

I attest and affirm….

Grace

Romans 12:3

> For by the grace given to me I say to everyone among you not to think of himself more highly than he ought to think, but to think with sober judgment, each according to the faith that God has assigned.

I attest and affirm...

I will use the grace that is given to me and walk in elegance and let all my movement be pleasing to the Lord. No matter how far I go in life I will always remember where I have come from and be grateful for where I have been. I will bring people up with me, sing the Lords praise for all that I am blessed with.

I will not think of myself as better than anyone else because I am a child of God, and we are all children of God. I am fearfully and wonderfully made, and I will rejoice in all my imperfections, because I am perfect in the eyes of the Lord. Even though I am an individual, I am an important part to the body of Christ. I have an important function in the body of Christ and understand that those standing beside me are also have important functions in the body of Christ and we should all work together for the good of the Kingdom.

I am the head and not the tail, I am above and not below, and I will remain humble in knowing that Christ created us all in his image and his likeness. I have a gift that may be different according to the grace that grace that God has given me, and when I join my gift with others, we become more powerful for the kingdom of the Lord.

I have an extremely important assignment, and I will always hold doing my Father's work in high regard, so I will continually pray reverently, listen patiently, and ask the Lord to provide me with the clarity that I need, so that I may fulfill my calling using sober judgment, a genuine heart, and humility as I continue along my days.

Amalia Lewis

Patience

1 Corinthians 13:4-8

> Love is patient, love is kind, it does not boast, it is not proud. It does not dishonor others, it is not self-seeking, it is not easily angered, it keeps no records of wrongs. Love does not delight in evil but rejoices with the truth. It always protects, always trusts, always hopes, always perseveres.

I attest and affirm...

Learning how to be patient is within my reach. It has been one of my more difficult lessons. I'm called, "Speedy Gonzales," by several of my friends, because I'm a fast mover. I like things to get done as swiftly and efficiently as possible. However, God wants us to be patient and wait on him to deliver the outcome the way he wants to deliver it.

I've missed Gods blessings plenty of times, because I was moving too fast. When I begin noticing my brain is on over-drive, I unplug myself from this loud crazy matrix we're in and I go somewhere quiet. This allows me time to listen to God's calling on my life. God knows when I need a break and suddenly an event comes up and away, I go for self-care and spa treatments. Sitting quiet and still is the precursor to learning patience.

I've also stood in shame before God knowing I was holding onto resentment and anger. If love is not easily angered, why do so many suffer from this? Once the pain is felt, the energy needs a new life source; and so, the cycle continues. Hurt people don't necessarily want to hurt others, I believe they want to release that negative energy that wasn't voluntarily taken.

The only true love that exist in this world is God's love. I've learned that if I can't always love myself, how can I fully love anyone else. We must first learn to love God and let him lead our path. Once we understand this level of love, we can begin loving ourselves, our partners and our children. We must understand that only through God, can love rain down to his children.

Ke'sha Dennis

Healing

Psalms 6:2

O Lord, heal me, for my bones are shaking with terror." When you are overwhelmed whether it is by physical, spiritual or emotional forces attacking you, remember the Bible speaks of miraculous healing through the work of Jesus Christ and faith in God. Our Lord can provide comfort and healing for all of us.

I attest and affirm...

When you become overwhelmed with health problems, bad news or any type of struggles, God's words can help ease your pain. God promises he has great things in store for us, we just must ask him. Praying to God is a good way to remind us of his promises that great things are to come. One organization has clarified this by interpreting the Prayer of Jabez. All about Prayer.org provides us with this: In the Old Testament Chronicles 4:9-10, it says:

> And Jabez called on the God of Israel, saying, "Oh that Thou would bless me indeed, and enlarge my coast, and that Thine hand might be with me, and that Thou would keep me from evil, that it may not grieve me!" And God granted him that which he requested.

This prayer reminds us that everybody struggles with choosing to rely on their self or God bless me indeed, and enlarge my coast, and that Thine hand might be with me, and that you would keep me from evil, that it may not grieve me!" And God granted him that which he requested.

This is a very important prayer because it shows us that Jabez understands what many people do not. There is only one God and He should be the center of our works God wants to bless every life. However, God wants us to first invite him into our lives and ask for his blessings. I tell you beloved, God hears your cries as well as your prayers. Proverbs 16:3 says "Commit thy works unto the Lord, and thy thoughts shall be established." No matter how bad your mind would have you believe there is no circumstance that God will not forgive. Whatever the situation is, he is with you, you just must call upon him.

Maureen Brewster

Psalms 6:2

O Lord, heal me, for my bones are shaking with terror." When you are overwhelmed whether it is by physical, spiritual or emotional forces attacking you, remember the Bible speaks of miraculous healing through the work of Jesus Christ and faith in God. Our Lord can provide comfort and healing for all of us.

I attest and affirm….

_____
_____
_____
_____
_____
_____
_____
_____
_____
_____
_____
_____
_____
_____
_____
_____

Expectations

Jeremiah 29:11

> For I know the thoughts I think toward you saith the Lord thoughts of peace, and not of evil, to give you an EXPECTED end.

I attest and affirm...

You are right in God's eyes, you are God's child, you are chosen, you are loved, you are more than a conqueror, you are a masterpiece of God, you are victorious, you are favored, and you are free.

Freedom and empowerment come when you obtain peace. I mean the peace that surpasses all understanding. When we are tried, and stretched out of our comfort zone we begin to create all kinds of excuses, illusions of negative thoughts that fuel in our minds, and we allow a doorway called fear to invite us in.

I remember when I was a baby in Christ operating in selfish and worldly ways. I could only see myself as a single mother, a failure to my children, a failure to myself, and failure to my mother. I saw things that looked to me as not picture perfect, but God's thoughts of me are of peace and unconditional love.

The moment I committed to building a relationship with God and his word my thoughts began to shift, and my eyes began to see things clearly. I could now see God's plan for my future, and they are to prosper me and you. We always think the worst of our situations placing limitations according to our own thoughts. The enemy will attack our minds and use our areas of weakness to break us and turn us away from God, but I decree and declare that on today you will use your weaknesses as opportunities to do better, and to be better steward over your life. We are the light created perfectly in his image from his DNA. Go out into the world and make the world happy. Do not wait on the world to make you happy. Let your light shine brightly from the mountain top above. God's thoughts of us will always be of peace to give us an expected end!

Carol Terrell

Gratitude

Psalm 118:24

>This is the day which the LORD has mad; Let us rejoice and be glad in it.

I attest and affirm...

I will be grateful for this day with enthusiasm. Once upon a time not long ago, I will confess and say that I did not always appreciate the beginnings of a new day. While I was happy to be among the living as the dawn gave way to a fresh day, I cannot say that I recognized how blessed I was to be able to "rejoice in it."

It wasn't until I witness someone who valued life and planned to grow old on earth, be given an expiration timeframe on his life. That someone would be my father. To watch someone, want to live but not be able to do so gave me a different perspective about cherishing each and every day that I rose.

Watching a life slowly leave this earthly realm humbled me to the core. I learned to relax and take things as they came despite any troubling events taking place around me; learned to embrace each day confessing and believing; learned to enjoy the present. I learned to stop postponing my "rejoice" and intentionally aimed at celebrating life daily.

I began to appreciate the rain; the sun; the snow; the hot and cold temperatures; the noise; the quiet; the failed plan; the success of completed goal; the good times and the bad times.

I began to pay more attention to my inner chat and stopped filling in the blanks with "when this happens I will ____" and began being more content with who, what, and where I currently was while on my journey to where I envisioned, I should be.

I learned that THIS day is the day to rejoice and be glad no matter what is going on or what will happen tomorrow, next week, next month or next year.

Twanda Grey

Psalm 118:24

This is the day which the LORD has mad; Let us rejoice and be glad in it.

I attest and affirm….

Jealousy

1 Peter 2:1

> Put away all malice and all deceit and hypocrisy and envy and all slander.

I attest and affirm...

You will be happy for people. You will celebrate and be motivated by them, instead of "wishing it were you". You will take responsibility for the success story you create for yourself. The key is this: It starts within. Your inner happiness, ambitious efforts and commitment will get you everything that you deserve.

Many times, we can become envious of others with no real reason. We pray for things and see other people get those exact same prayers answered, while we do not. Yet, we don't consider what it could have taken for them to get it in the first place. We don't consider the fact that they may have had challenges and setbacks to get it. I'm beginning to realize that a lot of things these days are all "smoke and mirrors. Everything it not what is seems. A lot of things that seem real are fake. A lot of happiness is sadness wrapped in pretty packages. In an era where we can nip and tuck and photoshop everything, you can't always hide the truth.

Jealousy is unhealthy and unnecessary. You'd be surprised at how people can be afraid of your confidence, your inner peace, your relationships and more. I challenge you to monitor all that you must be grateful for. Believe it or not, you have a lot. Many of us forget that somewhere else in this world, many do not have their essential daily needs. If it's material things that give you the most joy, then your priorities aren't in order. Express gratitude and count your blessings because there are people who would kill to be in your shoes.

You may think you don't have enough and someone, somewhere is jealous of you. Pray for them. You have a lot. You are rich in comparison to many, even with the bare minimum. Everything isn't always what it seems. Pray for your neighbors, daily. Especially the ones you may despise or envy. Behind closed doors they may live in misery. Many times, we see the cars, the home, the career and relationships and forget that we only see from our lens. I bet if God changed your eye prescription, you'd be surprised at what you really see. You have nothing to envy and no reason to be deceitful. Let people be who they are and pray for them. You never know how your prayer can be the biggest blessing.

Serita Love

Comfort

2 Cor 1:4

He comforts us in all our troubles.

I attest and affirm...

My story is filled with broken pieces, bad choices, and nasty truths. It's also filled with a major comeback, peace in my soul, new mercies, and grace that saved my life. Whenever you do not understand what is happening in your life, just get down on your knees, bow your head, close your eyes, take a deep breath and say " God, I know it's your plan, just help me through it."

God gave us the gift of life, but it is up to us to give ourselves the gift of living well. For every time that you think you are being rejected, denied, turned down God is redirecting your path, and ordering your steps in the direction of something better. Our troubles do not last always, we do have to grow through the process. We must stop seeking thoughts and opinions from others while we are in the storm. I say this because our thoughts are not his thoughts, and even though we may not mean anyone harm our advice could be delaying the recovery process of others, prolonging their breakthrough.

Do not worry about other people's opinion of you. God did not put you on this earth to impress people, only to love them. Disappointments are just God's way of saying now is the not the time. I have something better. Never be afraid to trust an unknown future to an ever-present God. While you are growing through your troubles, he is a God of comfort, just reach out and extend your hand and he will grab it and hold on to it.

Every day that you wake up is a gift from God. Do not take that for granted while you are complaining about your troubles. There is no guarantee of a tomorrow, so see the good of this day and make the very best of it. The hardest battles are given to God's strongest soldiers, so hold your head up high stick out your chest and extend your shoulders Queen because you are not easily broken, you are resilient, and with God's comfort all things are possible.

Carol Terrell

Wisdom

Proverbs 3:13-14

Blessed is the one who finds wisdom, and the one who gets understandings, for the gain from her is better than gain from silver and her profit better than gold.

I attest and affirm...

I will seek knowledge and understanding, as I know that the fear of the Lord is the beginning of knowledge. I will fear the Lord and keep all commandments. I will be wise to know to love wisdom and instruction. I will listen attentively as you pour your spirit into me, and I will heed your words. I will meditate on your word daily, and listen to hear your voice to dwell secure, and be at ease in times of disaster, for I know that you are in control.

I will receive your commandments and lend an attentive ear to wisdom. I understand that wisdom comes from the Lord, and from his mouth comes knowledge and understanding. I will walk in integrity and guard the path of justice. Through understanding and knowledge, gain wisdom into my heart and there I will hold your treasures, which is the word of the Lord.

I know that when wisdom is in my heart, it is then that I am truly blessed. The earth was founded by wisdom, and the Heavens were established by understanding. I will not lose sight of the work that I am meant to accomplish on earth, and I will walk upright and not stumble. Wisdom is better than silver and gold therefore I know the treasure that I have in my heart.

Through knowledge and understanding I will not forsake the Lord's teachings. They will forever be with me, and I will spread the wisdom that I have inside of me to all that will listen. I will ensure that the words that I speak are pleasing to your ears, that I may be blessed all the days of my life.

For you have taught me the way of wisdom and led me to the path of righteousness. I will keep all instruction, and I will not let go of her, as I will guard with my life. For you are the truth, the way, and the life, forever.

Amalia Lewis

Proverbs 3:13-14

Blessed is the one who finds wisdom, and the one who gets understandings, for the gain from her is better than gain from silver and her profit better than gold.

I attest and affirm....

_____
_____
_____
_____
_____
_____
_____
_____
_____
_____
_____
_____
_____
_____
_____
_____
_____

Transformed

Romans 12:2

> Do not conform to the pattern of this world but be transformed by the renewing of your mind. Then you will be able to test and approve what God's will is-his good, pleasing and perfect will.

I attest and affirm...

I will live a life that is transformed, not conformed, by the renewing of my mind. Changing the way you think changes your perspective which changes how you act in the world. Having a negative perspective about life can be draining! Take every thought captive and examine the source. Capturing your thoughts requires stillness.

Faulty thinking and negative thoughts of fear, bitterness, guilt, discouragement, resentment, unforgiveness to name a few steals our energy. Some of the most energy draining kinds of thoughts are those about failures, fear of making changes and past mistakes. And the fact of the matter is if it has come to past, we cannot do anything about it anyways. Learn from the situation or circumstance and focus forward. We can think about the past and what we have lost, or we can think about the future and the opportunities that we can aim towards.

Negative thoughts create negative emotions which creates negative moods. You can break this cycle in your life. When you have a problem, nothing negative will fix it. Keep your mind, mouth, moods and attitudes positive.

What you allow into your mind determines your reality and ultimately your legacy. We can choose which way we think! It is a choice that we have control of.

This scripture says it best:

> Do not be anxious about anything, but in everything by prayer and supplication with thanksgiving let your requests be made known to God. And the peace of God, which surpasses all understanding, will guard your hearts and your minds in Christ Jesus. Finally, brothers, whatever is true, whatever is honorable, whatever is just, whatever is pure, whatever is lovely, whatever is commendable, if there is any excellence, if there is anything worthy of praise, think about these things. Philippians 4:6-8

Controlling your thoughts is a process. Don't give up! Continue claiming what belongs to you (your mind and your thinking belong to you).

Twanda Grey

Miracles

Luke 12:48

> For unto whomsoever much is given, of him shall be much required.

I attest and affirm...

I will forever sing praises unto your name God. If you never do anything else Lord you have already done enough. You have given me peace, love, joy, happiness, wisdom, knowledge, understanding, wealth with options, and an intimate relationship with you. To whom much is given much is required. I just want to encourage someone that the word much does not mean monetary. Your blessing's come in many ways. There are couples out here that can never have their own children but have been afforded the opportunity to adopt. There are people in the world that are without sight or hearing, but they have their arms and legs. There are handicap people in the Olympics winning medals. There are musicians who cannot even read but they are writing music for some of the top artists. We often use the word much out of context. What I mean is we are expecting monetary miracles when God is a God that affords wealth with options. Every blessing does not have to be in the form of money or riches. If you have the activity of your limbs consider yourself to have much, if you can see and hear consider that to be much, and if you have your sense of taste consider that to be much. There are so many millionaires that are unhappy, mentally messed up, on drugs, and committing suicide because they have no peace, they are without love, they have lost their understanding, and they have no family. All they have is their money, their bad decision making, their selfishness, and people who are only around them for their lifestyle of the rich and famous status. We fall prey to worldly monetary things forgetting about how much has been afforded to us that is not monetary and that is irreplaceable. God has already done so much for us when he gave his only begotten son for our sins. We owe him so much in return. Look back over your life and remember a time when something great happened in your life that you did not expect, and you said didn't nobody do this but God. If that is all he ever has done for you he has already done enough. He has ordered our steps, he continues to direct our paths, he continues to pour into our cups until they run over, he continues to afford us Much, and we continue to give him little. Look back over your life and look at where you are on today and give God a Glory Hallelujah for what he has already done. It may look small to us, but God is a five-course meal preparer. He never gives us ala carte results so let's stop giving him ala carte praises.

Carol Terrell

Luke 12:48

For unto whomsoever much is given, of him shall be much required.

I attest and affirm….

Karma

Proverbs 20:22-23

> Don't say, "I will get even for this wrong." Wait for the Lord to handle the matter. The Lord detests double standard; he is not pleased by dishonest scales.

I attest and affirm...

My mission is to change my mindset about hurt and allow God to replace the hurt with healing and forgiveness. It can be difficult and may take years or even decades, but we're called by God to release our cares and burdens upon him. With releasing the pain, there's a sense of freedom we should all experience. Life becomes lighter and you feel a sense of freedom.

How many times have you been wronged? How many times have you wanted to make that person hurt as bad as they've hurt you? Majority of us have either acted out this thought, or we've thought about doing it. Either way both are sins. We are supposed to ask the Lord to take care of the situation for us. However, God's timing and our timing are set on two different time zones. We tend to want the perpetrator to hurt immediately after they've hurt us. We must patiently wait on the Lord and trust that he will do as he has promised, by making our enemy our footstool.

We are all held accountable for our own sins. Although we may have been wronged, we are called to wait on God to deliver us from our pain. Karma doesn't miss. She is always collecting her debt. Whether she comes that year or ten years later, understand that she'll show up. When we attack the perpetrator for hurting us, we too have opened the door for karma to enter our lives. The cycle will continue, until someone trusts God.

Ke'sha Dennis

Strength

Philippians 4:13

I can do all things through him who strengthens me.

Isaiah 41:10-13

Beloved, who do you rely on for inner strength? 'Fear not, for I am with you; be not dismayed, for I am your God; I will strengthen you. I will help you; I will uphold you with my righteous hand. Behold, all who are incensed against you shall be put to shame and confounded; those who strive against you shall be as nothing and shall perish. You shall seek those who contend with you, but you shall not find them; those who war against you shall be nothing at all. For I, the Lord your God, hold your right hand; it is I who say to you, "Fear not, I am the one who helps you."

I attest and affirm...

I have received God's help and it has strengthened me at some of my darkest and trying times. There were times when my enemies tried to destroy my reputation, career and family. God whispered to me, "They cannot destroy that which I have given you." Let me tell you, I lifted my head up, straighten my crown, checked myself in the mirror and spoke to my reflection in the mirror these words, "I am a Soldier in the mightiest Army in existence, I am a Soldier in God's army, and no weapon formed against me shall prosper." Every night and morning I say those words, they are my daily mantra.

There are days when it seems like a heavy load is weighing me down and I am sure you, Beloved have felt the same way. I am here to remind you; he is with you as he is with me. He strengthens us all, we just must be mindful to call on him. There may be times when you feel weary and do not want to go on, that's when God needs you the most. He wants us to bring our troubles to him because whoa, he got something planned for our enemies and what is so smooth about it, he plans it accordingly that our enemies don't even know what happened or why?

Beloved, what is ailing you, give it to God, communicate with him. He will not disappoint you.

Maureen Brewster

Calling

Philippians 3: 13-14

> Brethren, I count not myself to have apprehended: but this one thing I do, forgetting those things which are behind, and reaching forth unto those things which are before. I press toward the mark for the prize of the high calling of God in Christ Jesus.

I attest and affirm...

Your past does not determine your future. I have had some trials, some tribulations, and some failures which I let eat away at me over some time. The light inside of me began to dim. I had no desire or drive to get out of bed some days. I faked the motions when my children were present but would cry when they were not around. I started calling out, crying out to God the comforter. I felt something in my spirit ignite and I began to regain my will power to get up, to fight, to press toward the mark for the prize of the highest calling of God. I encourage you not to live in your past, but instead embrace it because your past disappointments are in fact your healing, your recovery, the chapters to your book, and your testimonies. You are God's chosen child beautifully and wonderfully made in his image. He will never remind you of your past or hold it over your head, He uses your past trials, tribulations, and failures as a toolbox to equip you for your future because without the toolbox we could never rebuild the blueprint. Your past is your story, it is what made you strong and whole again, it is what ministers to the hurt, the broken, the weak, the sick, the one who is ready to give up, and the one who has given up on God. It is the prize of the high calling of our God in Christ Jesus.

Carol Terrell

Anger

Psalm 37: 8

Don't give in to worry or anger; it only leads to trouble.

I attest and affirm...

Anger will not live in your spirit. You will get upset from time to time, but you will practice self-control. No, things aren't always going your way and people aren't always going to behave in the manner that you prefer, but you won't let that get to you. With God's grace, you will master the art of being calm when you're being tested. You will not give in.

Being angry can throw you completely off your square. You will get sidetracked and mismanage the things that are most important to you. You deserve better than that! So, if it's a romantic partner, a co-worker, a neighbor or loved one –you will not allow them to dictate how you feel. Instead of focusing on problems, you will focus on solutions. Instead of being confused, you will focus on gaining a better understanding when you simply don't understand what's happening around you. Your increased level of emotional intelligence will be the Master Key to your success of keeping the peace when you want war.

There are people who know how to push buttons, but if your "angry button" is out of order, then their attempts won't work. You can't control what happens in your life, but God allow us to master how we respond and that is powerful.

Serita Love

Positivity

Proverbs 8: 6-7

> Hear, for I will speak noble things, and from my lips will come what is right, for my mouth will utter truth, wickedness is an abomination to my lips.

I attest and affirm...

I will speak positively and live a positive life. When I say things, I will say them I a way that is pleasing to the lord. The tongue is a powerful weapon, and words are very powerful. Life and death lie in the power of the tongue and I want to speak life into all that come into my life and see then prosper and do great work for the kingdom of God.

I am the sower, and it is my duty to sow that word, so that I can produce a fruitful seed for the kingdom of God. People will not always remember your face or where they met you, however they will remember what you did and what you said. I will be remembered for the life that I speak, and my actions that are pleasing to my Father. I will encourage those around me with my words, to do better, the make something of themselves. I will leave a legacy that my Father in Heaven is proud of.

I always want to be justified by the words that I speak, and not condemned by my words. I will choose what is right so that the words that are tasted by the pallet of mouth are sweet, and not bitter. I am slow to anger, and slow to speak, so that I gain wisdom and understanding by listening, and am then mindful of my words. I will ensure my mind is focused on you to make decisions based on what you have for my life.

I will not take head to words that are not positive, nor will I let negativity enter my thoughts if they are ever spoken into my life, and I will forever pray for a fruitful life that it pleasing to you using my mind, body, and spirit. For you are the truth, the way, and the life.

Amalia Lewis

Proverbs 8: 6-7

Hear, for I will speak noble things, and from my lips will come what is right, for my mouth will utter truth, wickedness is an abomination to my lips.

I attest and affirm....

Loyalty

Proverbs 19: 22-23

Loyalty makes a person attractive. It is better to be poor than dishonest. Fear of the Lord leads to life, bringing security and protection from harm.

I attest and affirm...

A person that stands in the truth of loyalty is attractive. An authentic loyal person is hard to come by these days. Times have changed drastically, and the world has a lot if cyber life people, who believe the internet is reality. People are living a lie daily, because the reality of their truth hurts too much more than living a lie. It's beginning to feel like we're living in a fake sense of reality and if you're too real you're looked at as the bad guy. Unfortunately, this has made the real and loyal people scarce in society.

A loyal person doesn't conform to societies rules. Loyal people live a different lifestyle that comes from a different code. God calls us to remain loyal to him and stand in our truth. Loyalty is a gift that God gives his special children and we must please God, by abiding by his laws and remaining loyal to him always. When we put our trust in man, we're setting ourselves up for disappointment. When we're loyal to God, we can also be loyal to those around us by living out his word. Temptation is always around God's loyal children. However, our strength to fight off those demons comes from God, so pray during rough times.

When we understand Gods word, we're held to a different standard than other people. Fearing the Lord means understanding the consequences of breaking his laws. There's a certain set of morals and ethics we must adhere to, because the consequences of doing the opposite can be catastrophic. Although I fear God, I rest assured that he'll always remain comforting in my time of need. I love the fact that I can call on him to rescue me anytime I'm going through something and he's right there to rescue me.

Ke'sha Dennis

Vision

Habakkuk 2:2-3

Then the Lord replied: "Write down the revelation and make it plain on tablets so that a herald may run with it. For the revelation awaits an appointed time, it speaks of the end and will not prove false. Though it lingers, wait for it; it will certainly come and will not delay."

I attest and affirm...

No matter the circumstances, your prayers and cries are being heard. This is the purpose of vision boards. When you create a vision board it become the herald or as interpreted the messenger. Luke, 11:9 states, "So I say to you: Ask and it will be given to you; seek and you will find; knock and the door will be opened to you." For everyone who asks receives; he who seeks finds; and to him who knocks, the door will be opened.

As children we are always asked, what do you want to be when you grow up? However, what we want to be and what our parents dictate we should become are not always the same. I am quite sure you have heard of the purpose driven life. Not many people can connect to their purpose. Some seek it out, trying to discover it and some succeed. I say this to you,

Beloved. Keep on asking, and you will receive what you ask for. Keep on seeking, and you will find. Keep on knocking, and the door will be opened to you.

I am not saying it will be easy, what I am saying is that you must be faithful to the process. Write your needs down on paper. Every night before bed, pray for what's on your list. Envision yourself having it as you fall asleep. When you awake, pray and thank God for allowing you another day of life and for another opportunity to receive his gifts. God's time is different from man, but when God does show up, he is always right on time. There will be times of struggle, but do not lose hope. The joy of the Lord is upon you. Just invite him in and I know he will come. Remember, "Ask and it shall be given to you."

Maureen Brewster

Discipline

Proverbs 12:1

> Whoever loves discipline loves knowledge, but whoever hates correction is stupid.

I attest and affirm...

You will have discipline. We all have desires. Things that many of us are not willing to work for. That successful business. That happy marriage. World Travel. Peace of mind. I can go on and on. You must be willing to work for what you want.

So many of us lack discipline. I'm guilty, yet I yearn to gain the wisdom and knowledge to redirect me to the main reason I want to have it in the first place. I wrote in my first book that discipline has rewards. If you work hard and smart, you get results. When you stick to a routine, your life gets easier and less stressful. Maintaining a disciplined life is powerful, because it puts most people at ease.

Just think about it. If you were more disciplined, you probably would have more money and you would even look and feel better. Lie wouldn't be in such disarray. Discipline doesn't allot chaos. Discipline is quiet and it is also orderly. Discipline requires something of us that many of us do not enjoy and that is criticism. To live a disciplined life, there will have to be some sort of accountability at the table. This doesn't mean that someone will ridicule you, but you will receive feedback and constructive input in your life. You must welcome this.

If discipline is not welcomed in your life, then you will aimlessly coast from one day to another with no clear direction. Discipline provides clarity. To create and reach goals that are attainable, one has to be disciplined. There's no way around it. If you truly want what you want out of this life, you will create what you need to get it. That thing that you need is discipline. I haven't fully mastered this, but I'm close. Therefore, I am speaking from experience. I pray that you get what you're looking for. Master the process of executing with discipline and I believe it shall be yours.

Serita Love

Proverbs 12:1

Whoever loves discipline loves knowledge, but whoever hates correction is stupid.

I attest and affirm….

Goodness

Galatians 6:9

> And let us not grow weary of doing good, for in due season we will reap, if we do not give up.

I attest and affirm...

I will not grow weary of doing well, as I know where my help, and my strength come from. I do not do anything in my life to be pleasing in the eyes of people. I do the work of the Lord to be pleasing in his eyes. I will not brag or boast about the work that I am doing, it is done purely out of love. With a genuine heart, and a kind spirit, as love is kind, it does not have an ego, and it does not brag or boast. I will sow positive prosperous seeds, with joy and gladness, as I know what they will become, and have faith of a mustard seed that the Lord is guiding my hands, and my heart that are all at work in his name. I am not looking for words of appreciation or owed anything. As all that I work for is done in the name of the kingdom of God, and I know that he sees me, and knows my name.

When my seeds have grown and begin to work in the Fathers names, I will give all the honor and glory to him, for he has given me guidance and wisdom and all the tools that I needs to be successful and finish his work. I will not finish until all the work is complete. If I ever feel tired, or restless I will pray to the father because he is where my strength and my help comes from. I will not give up, no matter how hard I think it is getting or how tired I feel because the feeling is only temporary, and the reward will be more far reaching than the work I am doing. I will do everything in gladness and thank the Lord in advance for giving me opportunities to do his work.

Amalia Lewis

Learning

Proverbs 17:16

It is senseless to pay tuition to educate a fool, since he has no heart for learning.

I attest and affirm...

I will move on with God's mission despite the fools. Fools come in all different shapes and forms. There are many fools living amongst us in the world today. People with no sense are walking around as if they know beyond a shadow of doubt, they're right and they couldn't be more wrong. God says for us not to argue with fools. I've made the mistake of participating in disagreements I know I'm right in. When we engage in disagreements with people who aren't willing to listen and learn, we're wasting our time and energy. Continuously going back and forth does neither party any good. The only outcome from arguing with a fool is unhappiness and frustration. Allow God to handle those situations for you.

There are people in the world who thirst for knowledge. There are others who don't want to learn anything from anyone. A fool has no desire to learn anything a teacher has to offer. These people will even become angry, if you try to correct anything, they're doing incorrect. This is the type of person who will drain you, if you allow them too. I've had people close to me tell me they choose to remain ignorant. They said it to me. From that moment on, I realized that regardless of who the fool is to you; let go and let God. Don't let them bring down your moral and continue to teach those willing to listen and learn. In this realization you may lose friends and family, but a fool is a fool, regardless of title.

I challenge everyone reading this to let go of those around you that you're feeding life into, but they'll never receive or understand what you have to offer. Move on with God's mission and tell your testimony to those willing to learn. There are so many people in the world who need to hear your story, but we're feeding all our life sources into the wrong people. Go out into the world and speak to someone who'll be encouraged. It feels good helping someone who appreciates it.

Ke'sha Dennis

Proverbs 17:16

It is senseless to pay tuition to educate a fool, since he has no heart for learning.

I attest and affirm….

Joy

James 1:2-3

> Consider it pure joy, my brothers and sisters, whenever you face trials of many kinds, because you know that the testing of your faith produces perseverance.

I attest and affirm...

You will prevail. You will be tested. Nothing about the game of life is fair. It's a game that everyone dies in, in the end. So, how do we make it count? Well, the best thing I can tell you is this: Every day will not be a good day. I'm not telling you anything new right now but let me say this: A bad DAY is not a BAD life.

Perseverance will be a major key to your life's success story. Many say that you can have it all, just not all at once. That statement speaks to me. When you believe you can have more, you figure out what it takes to get it. Most of the time, our thoughts include things that God wants us to have. We just must work for it. We must stay strong. We must have joy even when we don't have the tangible or intangible things that make us proud.

You are going to be tested from so many angles in life. Tests with your jobs, relationships, health, state of mind and more. All these things have the potential to make you or break you and it's up to you to defy the odds. As you are tested, you must keep in mind who you decide to become on the other side of adversity. Will you rise to the occasion and blow your own mind, or will you fold?

When you realize that there are great things waiting for you on the other side of fear, I believe that you will come out on top in the end. Have joy, even in time of difficulty. Yes, it's easier said than done. We don't think about joy after heartbreak, losing a job or loved one or getting bad news. That's the thing. We need to think about it. Joy is the light at the end of the tunnel. We simply must imagine what it's like to have joy when we get there, before we get there. You deserve Joy. I pray that you always keep it.

Serita Love

Genuineness

Romans 12:9-10

Let love be genuine. Abhor what is evil; hold fast to what is good. Love one another with brotherly affection.

I attest and affirm...

I will love with genuineness and sincerity. I will stray away from what is evil and hold to what is good. I will serve the Lord, be a servant to his people as well. I will bless those that persecute me, and I will not curse them. I am blessed to be a blessing, and I know that you are in control, and will never let my enemies defeat me.

The only way to drive out hate is through love, and I will love with all my heart, and give of my own free will. I will be kind to others, I will help those that are in need, and everything that I do, I will do it with a joyful heart. Those that have hatred in their heart I will love them anyway, I will help them anyway, because we are all children of God, and deserve to be loved.

My heart is filled with love, and kindness, and renounce what is evil. I won't hold grudges because God is a God of love. I will not repay evil with evil, nor an eye for an eye, as it does nothing but create confusion, and God is not a God of confusion. I know that the love that I have for God's people will keep me, and my genuine concern will be passed on through for generations, that they love God, and his people as I have. I hold fast in my heart and will pray that they as well have genuine love, abhor from what is evil, and hold fast always to what is good and what is just. The only thing that can drive out hate, and evil is love, and I will hold love in my heart for as long as I live.

Amalia Lewis

Love

1 Corinthians 13:13

> And now these three remain: faith, hope and love. But the greatest of these is love.

I attest and affirm...

You love all things that you encounter in life. It builds character and makes for a great story. Love your enemies. Love your lessons. Love your challenges. Hate is a powerful emotion, but love overrides all! Love is peaceful. Love is generous. Love heals so many wounds before they even appear in the first place. It you want ultimate peace, then love will be the answer.

Love your flaws. They make you unique. Love when things are difficult, because things can always get better or be better. When you love yourself, people mirror you with love and respect most of the time.

When I learned to love the process to the things I didn't understand, it made me a better woman. I became more determined to figure things out, because we don't know what we don't know. When you're under pressure, you either become a diamond or dust! The outcome, in most cases is up to you.

What makes love beautiful is the fact that it is a universal language. Whether you love gifts or like to give gifts, you can express it either way. Whether you like quality time or you like to be available for others, it's another way to express love. If it's through your words or if the words of others, make you feel loved, that is powerful. Love is in the touch form you or others, if it makes you feel comfortable or secure. Love is a gift that you can give an receive.

Love is more powerful than faith. Love is more powerful than hope. Love is something that we all can put out to the universe to make this world a better place. If you do nothing else, make it your business to do most things with love. It may change your entire life!

Serita Love

Praise

Psalms 59:16

But I will sing of your strength; I will sing aloud of your steadfast love in the morning. For you have been to me a fortress and a refuge in the day of my distress.

I attest and affirm...

I will always sing your praises and speak of the strength that you give me every day. I will give you the same energy each day of my life. I will read your world and hold on to its teachings. I will hold your word in my heart, so that when I need it, it is always with me.

The days can be long, and so can the nights, but if I have you by my side, I am victorious. There may be times where I feel like I won't make it, or I have doubt of where my help comes from. Yet, I will always reflect and be rest assured that my help comes from you, my strength comes from you, and that brings me joy every day.

You have been there from the beginning and you never fail me. You are always right on time when I need you most. I can move any mountain, and weather any storm for I am victorious, and you know what I need. You provide me with the tools I need to succeed, and your word has a word for every life lesson that I will face. I will sing to the high skies and let everyone know that is listening, just how good you are, and how much you love me, and care for me.

You are my strength and I will suit up in the armor of God each and every day of my life. I will make sure I wear the helmet of salvation, the breastplate of righteousness, the belt of truth, sword of the spirit, the shield of faith, and the feet of peace. I will sing of your strength because I am strong in the Lord, and in the power of your might!

Amalia Lewis

Psalms 59:16

But I will sing of your strength; I will sing aloud of your steadfast love in the morning. For you have been to me a fortress and a refuge in the day of my distress.

I attest and affirm....

Friendship

Proverbs 17:17

A friend loves at all times.

I attest and affirm...

You will continue to acquire friends on your journey ahead. Far too often I state that "most people haven't even met their best friends yet." This statement is true for those of us who evolve and must leave some "friends" behind. Friends that last a lifetime stay on course. They are loving, kind, support and they hold you accountable for your actions. They love by being honest. They love by being there when it matters most. They are supportive. They tell "hard truths". Friends love you through the ups and downs. They respect you. They check on you. They call you out when you are out of character and out of line, respectfully.

Friends grow with you. They become a tool and resource as needed, because you need each other. Friends don't allow anyone to disrespect and place dirt on your name. If they bear witness to such debauchery, they clean it up for your name sake. Maybe I am speaking of the type of friend I have grown to love and become. I wasn't always the best friends with others, because I wasn't a great friend with myself. Sometimes, you must learn how to love correctly, after witnessing people be loved improperly.

Sometimes, you must heal yourself, before passing your pain onto others like a virus. Sometimes, you must let God work on you. When you discover the friend within, you will be able to love at a level beyond your understanding. This happens, because you're capable; It happens because you're lovable. It happened because you deserve to be a great friend and attract them as you grow. If a friend always loves, then real love starts with love within. To have great friends, start with the friend with in. Be your own bestie, first. Everything else will be a bonus.

Serita Love

Proverbs 17:17

A friend loves at all times.

I attest and affirm….

_____
_____
_____
_____
_____
_____
_____
_____
_____
_____
_____
_____
_____
_____
_____
_____
_____
_____
_____
_____

Light

Ephesians 5:8-9

> For at one time you were darkness, but now you are light in the Lord. Walk as children of light. For the fruit of light is found in all that is good and right and true.

I attest and affirm...

I am not my past, and that I have a bright present and an even brighter future in front of me through the Lord. Through his love, wisdom, and guidance. I was once in the darkness, but now I am walking in the light. I am a child of God, and my Father knows my name. He loved me so much that he sent his only begotten son to save the world and die for my sins that that I may walk in truth. I am not ashamed of the person that I was once was, as when my flesh died, it was washed away, and I was made new. I will use the time that I have here on earth to be a light to those that are in the dark and be a beacon of light for the world to see. Help them to see the goodness in themselves and see goodness in other people as well. My light shines ever so bright, and I will not allow anyone to dim the light that shines within me.

I know that there will be times where I will feel like I am alone, however I know that through your word, that I am not alone. I always have someone with me. When I am not able to shine my light bright enough or I feel that is it going them. I know that you are with me, and I have Angels surrounding me to help me. Angels with their own light that may have been in the darkness at one point in time. Angels come in many forms and share their light with the world as well. I will hold strong to your word, hold it in my heart and treasure it, so that my light will shine brightly no matter where I go.

Amalia Lewis

Service

Galatians 5:13-14

> You, my brothers and sisters, were called to be free. But do not use your freedom to indulge the flesh; rather, serve one another humbly in love. For the entire law is fulfilled in keeping this one command: "Love your neighbor as yourself.

I attest and affirm...

You will serve. One of the most amazing things that a human being can do on this planet is service our fellow men, women and children of the world! I fell in love with service a long time ago. Nothing gives me more joy that to help youth and guide our women and men.

When you understand the value of service, you quickly realize that God has you on assignment. We don't all get the same homework and that is what makes the class of life so beautiful. There are things that you will go through and grow through that will allow you to become the cheat sheet to the success of someone else. That person may be a stranger or a friend.

God equips you to serve and you must execute with pride. What makes leaders special is they simple do and they are led to by the grace and guidance of God. People need us. They may need a dollar, a home, a job, food or peace of me. It is you who will be that resource or guide. Unfortunate, you won't be capable of helping everyone, but you will be able to bless so many. Those of who you bless may pay it forward and keep your legacy moving forward.

You can do so many things for free that will change the lives of many. Volunteer your time, money or resources. Give someone a listening ear. Give back. Teach someone a new skill. Give someone a new opportunity. Speak hope into the ears of the hopeless. Lend a helping hand every change you get. When you serve, you get a better perspective on people, life, love and more.

I love to serve. I have a weak spot in my heart for the youth. I teach them and learn even more when we are together. I mentor and advocate for ambitious youth from underserved communities. All it takes is for one person to take a step forward. Doing so, makes that person an example. That person is me. That person is you. We are required to serve. God is pleased with those of us who serve.

Serita Love

Forward

Proverbs 4:25-26

> Let your eyes look directly forward, and your gaze be straight before you. Ponder the path of your feet; then all your ways will be sure.

I attest and affirm...

I will run my race, as no one will be able to run my race for me, I will not look to my left or to my right, but directly forward and let me eyes stay before me. I cannot compare myself, or my life to anyone else's because my life was given to me for a purpose, on purpose.

I will let my feet be sure as it goes on the path, as I know the Lord is with me and he gives me strength to so all things. I will fear no evil and I know that the Lord is watching over me, as I go through life doing my Father's work.

Nothing is impossible through Christ who strengthens me, and I know that the road may not always be easy, but I know that the path set for me is the path set by God for a reason. Any trial and tribulations I go through is for a reason, and whatever does not defeat me will only make me stronger.

I am placed on this earth to be a living testimony, and as I run my race I will speak of the Lord's goodness along the way and be a strong testament of faith. At times ever though I may only have the faith of a mustard seed, I will hold fast to the words of my father. I will always be sure of the promises of God. I know that whatever I go through is only temporary and I will not compare my temporary situation to anyone else's because God created it for me.

So I as go down a road less traveled, I pray for traveling mercy and your guidance for knowledge and understanding, because I know and have faith that you are with me all the days of my life and I trust in you and the have faith that you will guide and order my steps.

Amalia Lewis

Success

Proverbs 16:3

Commit to the Lord whatever you do, and your plans will succeed.

I attest and affirm...

You will succeed! I have always had the desire to succeed in life. Even when I had no idea what success looked like for me. My faith in the Lord, has revealed so many rewarding things. I just had to believe and do the work. Without the faith, you won't believe you can do anything. With the faith, you will believe you can do virtually everything. Trust your process. Trust your thoughts. Rid negative thoughts and know that you will be successful in your own right.

That commitment to the lord in all that you do is what will keep you on steady ground, when you are doubting yourself. It will fulfill you when you when you get stuck and just don't know what to do. Stay committed to being in alignment with what God has already co-signed on for you. Just like a car note, if you aren't committed to paying your monthly bill, that car will be taken away from you. You must have a clear plan and a strategy for that plan. Many times, you need to have a contingency plan, in case things don't work out.

Most times, when we are on course to succeed, we get a ton of detours. Detours still get you to your destination. Even with the potholes, inclement weather, accidents and rush hours, you must stay committed to where you are headed. It is already written that you will get there. Your actions, patience, resilience and grace will guarantee that you do. There is beauty in created your own success story. The adversity and criticism will come, but you will keep your eye on the prize. No one can take what has your name on it, so go out there and succeed.

Serita Love

Proverbs 16:3

Commit to the Lord whatever you do, and your plans will succeed.

I attest and affirm....

Love

1 Corinthians 13:13

So now faith, hope, and love abide, these three; but the greatest of these is love.

I attest and affirm...

I will have faith, hope, and above all else and abundance of love. I will have the faith to believe in God's promises, I will trust in his faithfulness, and rely on him in all matters concerning my life. I will have hope in the Lord so that my strength is continually renewed. God knows the plans he has for me, and to know that he has plans for me gives me hope for the future.

With hope in the Lord, I know that I will soar on wings like eagles, I will not grow weary, and I will not faint. I know that God's love has been poured out into my heart through the Holy Spirit, who he has given to us. I know that God is a God of hope; therefore, I am filled with joy and peace just knowing that my life is filled with hope.

My heart is filled with joy, happiness and love for God and God's people. I will rejoice in knowing the Fathers word and leaning not on my own understanding. I will spread the faith, and hope, and the love that I have. I will continually be kind and genuine to those that I encounter.

I pray to be able to find the words from the Lord to speak hope into my life and the lives of others. I have faith that The Lord and his Angels are watching over me each and every day, giving me the strength to do all things and be prosperous in the kingdom of Heaven.

I have faith in the things that I cannot see, and the hope that in knowing that God will always provide a way. Above all else I will have love in my heart for my neighbor, my brothers and sisters, and I will speak loving words because just as life and death are in the power of the tongue, with loving words, and actions anything is possible.

Amalia Lewis

Abundance

Mark 10:27

And Jesus looking upon them saith, with men it is impossible but not with God: for with God ALL THINGS ARE POSSIBLE.

I attest and affirm...

Your faith in God will produce a life of abundance. I speak health into your bodies, I speak love into your relationships, I speak wealth into your bank accounts, and I speak good measure, pressed down, shaken together, running over into everything you touch. When we take matters into our own hands, we limit ourselves from the blessings that God has for us. Our thoughts are not his thoughts and when we lean to our own understanding, we place ourselves in this space so small and so distant from what has already been predestined over our lives. Stop placing God in a box and sitting him on a shelf. Our God is bigger than a mountain, he is wider than a river, and he is deeper than a valley. Nothing is impossible for our God! Often, we act as the pilot of our life steering and guiding the wheel down all the wrong paths never seeking guidance or direction from our Father. Suddenly we find out that things become impossible in life because we are seeking direction from people. You must CHANGE THE INGREDIENTS if you want a different result. I have experienced many trials and tribulations that

I did not know would become my testimonies for his Glory! I have evolved into the Woman of God he has called me to be, embracing being a single mother, being homeless not once but twice with my children, an abusive marriage, insecurities, and brokenness. I am the Evolution of Woman, I Am She, I Am the 2023 version of me, I Am Phenomenally ME because with God ALL THINGS ARE POSSIBLE just try him and see!

    Carol Terrell

Agreement

Matthew 18:19

> Again, I say to you, if two of you agree on earth about anything they ask, it will be done for them by my Father in heaven.

I attest and affirm...

I will have faith that whatever I agree on here on earth will be done by my Father in heaven. I will surround myself with those that are uplifting and positive, so that we are able to make a positive change and do work in my Father's name.

Amalia Lewis

Matthew 18:19

Again, I say to you, if two of you agree on earth about anything they ask, it will be done for them by my Father in heaven.

I attest and affirm….

_____
_____
_____
_____
_____
_____
_____
_____
_____
_____
_____
_____
_____
_____
_____
_____
_____
_____
_____

Saints and Sinners

Luke 15: 1-4

> Now the tax collectors and sinners were all gathering around to hear Jesus. But the Pharisees and the teachers of the law muttered, "This man welcomes sinners and eats with them." Then Jesus told them this parable: "Suppose one of you has a hundred sheep and loses one of them. Doesn't he leave the ninety-nine in the open country and go after the lost sheep until he finds it?

I attest and affirm...

I deserve the redemption that my Father makes available to me. I have made mistakes and allowed myself to sulk in self-pity. I have been a victim of doing this. I avoided family and friends during this time for fear of disappointing them when the truth was: I was disappointed in myself. It is not easy trying to live up to the expectations of others. We are taught too, it is drilled into us at home, school and even on our jobs. With the help of the Holy Spirit whispering in my subconscious," there is nothing to fear"! I felt a rush of confidence rush of over and reminded myself to ask God for forgiveness, then ask my family and friends. How I felt a mighty weight lifted.

There are times when we put so much pressure on ourselves to live and become what others want us to be and forget we are who God created us to be. We tend to deviate from the plan God has for us. Some are fortunate to realize this and make their way back to God's original plan for their life. You, my beloved can too. It takes three things, faith, trust, and courage.

Faith in God, trust in God and the courage to begin. Seek and yea shall find the road to an abundant life our Father has for you.

Maureen Brewster

Sinner & Saint

Luke 15: 4-7

> And when he finds it, he joyfully puts it on his shoulders and goes home. Then he calls his friends and neighbors together and says, "Rejoice with me; I have found lost sheep." I tell you that in the same way there will be more rejoicing in heaven over one sinner who repents than over ninety- nine righteous persons who do not need to repent.

I attest and affirm...

Salvation is a work of God for man, rather than a work of man for God (Lewis Sperry Chafer). Thank you, God for you are our savior and redeemer, no child of God can sink so deep into a depression of sin that you cannot save them. Actress Marilyn Monroe, the heart of Hollywood was asked about her mental state in an interview. She responded with honesty that stunned those in listening distance. She said

> I need one of those long hugs where you kind of forget whatever else is happening around you for a minute.

I have had many friends and family members turn to alcohol and/or drugs (illegal and prescription) to deal with their depression. Some of them sought help through rehabilitation and others did not, those who did were redeemed. Beloved I say unto you, "Let not your heart be weary, for there are arms waiting to give you long hugs and welcome you home."

Like the prodigal son who squander his inheritance and was too ashamed to return home, a celebration is prepared for us regardless of your past choices and outcomes. When the prodigal son returned, his father held a feast and celebrated him. His father was worried that he was dead. He rejoiced because his son was alive. Your past sin doesn't define you. You still have a choice to move forward. You can return to the care of a loving father. Your life is what the Father celebrates.

Maureen   Brewster

God's Plan

Jeremiah 29:11

> For I know the plans I have for you declares the Lord, plans to prosper you and not to harm you. Plans to give you help and a future.

I attest and affirm...

I have gotten out of my own way! Too often we try to control our lives, only to find out how out of control our lives really are. Today I release fear, doubt and insecurities. Today I let go and let God. I've lost too many years believing I was in control of my own destiny and today I thank God for understanding he's in full control.

I thought I wanted to be a Registered Nurse, but God had something greater in store for me. I now own a financial consulting tax business and I've opened a financial resource non-profit by the name of Lady Buzz, Conversations that create movement. As I look back at how determined I was to become a registered nurse, I now realize I would've been so unhappy. This showed me that God knows better for me than I know for myself. I would've never dreamed the ordinary Berkeley, California girl would be making the connections I am making today.

God has made this world for his children. There is much fruit to be harvested. Our Father wants us to have a life of abundance. It's time for us to tap into the gifts he gave each one of us and go spread what God gave you across the world. We must believe in our gifts on those days we don't want to get out of the bed. We must tap into our gifts when we fear what the outside world will throw at us today, because God doesn't put more on us than we can bare. Do not allow fear to swallow your destiny. I demand that today you embrace peace, resilience, determination and drive. Today you will change your mindset and show up to embrace Gods will on your life.

Ke'sha Dennis

I Am No Longer Broken

Isaiah 43:2

> When you pass through the water, I will be with you; and when you pass through the rivers, they will not sweep over you. When you walk through the fire, you will not be burned; the flames will not set you ablaze.

I attest and affirm...

I am no longer broken. I am no longer bound by my negative thoughts, instead I am enriched by the promises of God that he will never leave nor forsake me. I am the head and not the tail, and I am the daughter of the King of Kings and Lord of Lords. I know what is not valuable to some is valuable in God's eyes.

I have been living in the past. Living through my attacks physically, spiritually, emotionally and mentally. I was beat down by people whom I trusted with my life and left to die, so it was a pain I was familiar with. I didn't know what my life was without the hurt and it started to feel good, now I at least felt something. For years I was so numb, shutdown and closed off from even the good people in my life. Being told I wouldn't amount to anything and I wouldn't be anybody in this world I started to believe every negative word spoken to me. My soul was fed so many lies that it stayed hungry for more, and it stayed full. I thought I wasn't good enough to be loved therefore I didn't love myself. Today it all stops.

Many have written me off, but I am the just and God is doing a new thing in me. I am no longer weak, because I am strong in the Lord. I have no choice but to count it all joy, because I am made in God's image and I am taking back what the devil thought he stole from me; My SELF-LOVE, My PEACE, My HEALTH, My HOPEFULNESS and My DIGNITY. Though I often find myself between a rock and a hard place, I know I am victorious, I am whole, and I AM RESTORED.

Ayeisha Latta-Matthews

Isaiah 43:2

When you pass through the water, I will be with you; and when you pass through the rivers, they will not sweep over you. When you walk through the fire, you will not be burned; the flames will not set you ablaze.

I attest and affirm….

I Am Encouraged

Philemon 1:20

> I do wish, brother, that I may have some benefit from you in the Lord; refresh my heart in Christ.

I attest and affirm...

I am encouraged. I pray the Lord Jesus surround me with true Brothers. In this case, surround me with sisters that will not only pray for me but bridge the gap when needed. I pray for true friends, honest business partners, and reassurance in the word.

Through my journey of entrepreneurship, I often get discouraged. In those times, I need reassurance. The best comes from trusted friends I lean on that will encourage me. When I fall, they aren't always present to pick me up. Yet they pray for me. They bridge the gap. They remind me of the goodness of the Lord when I need it.

I encourage you to find friends who are believers. I also encourage you to be that friend as well. As we are encouraged by our friends, you should be that friend to remind them where they come from. Remind them that all things are possible through Christ.

Some people listen to your problems because they like drama. And misery loves company. These people always end up stabbing you in the back or sharing your confidential information. You may start keeping stuff to yourself. You start internalizing your stress. You think you are going crazy. But you're not. You are not alone. I attest and affirm that in Christ you have friends.

Jade Cross-French

What to do with Your Life

Philemon 3: 13-14

> Brothers and sisters, I do not consider myself yet to have taken hold of it. But one thing I try to do is forgetting what is behind me and straining toward what is ahead, I press on toward the goal to win the prize for which God has called me heavenward in Christ Jesus.

I attest and affirm...

I am letting go of all things that I have allowed to hold me back, my past. For I know faith is not knowing what the future holds, but knowing who holds the future, (Anonymous). Sally Ozovech writes in her devotional, "The highest goal in your life is to conform to Christ." As I am looking forward, I will strive to do my part in making better use of the gifts God has given me. For faith without works is dead (James 2:26).

My prayer is punctuated by this type of working faith:

Lord, help me to achieve the goal that you have for my life. Guide me. Continue to strengthen me. For if I falter, my faith will provide all I need to strive forward and upward.

I am not saying it will be easy, change, real change of oneself never is but it is doable. No matter what religious tenet you follow or not, deciding what needs to change in your life and changing it is doable. You will need help; however, you first take a stand to change what is holding back from living, true living and discovering your divine driven purpose.

Magic happens when you do not give up even though you want to. When life pushes you down, it's testing you to see whether you have the strength or not to stand back up. One of the hardest decisions you'll ever make is choosing whether to walk away or try harder (curiano.com). Beloved, do not be afraid to seek help, you will be helping someone else too.

Maureen Brewster

Philemon 3: 13-14

Brothers and sisters, I do not consider myself yet to have taken hold of it. But one thing I try to do is forgetting what is behind me and straining toward what is ahead, I press on toward the goal to win the prize for which God has called me heavenward in Christ Jesus.

I attest and affirm….

Embracing His Will

Luke 12:48

To whom much is given, much will be required

I attest and affirm...

I will embrace HIS will for my life. There was a time in my life when I use to complain about the mundane and an enormous number of "things" that consumed my life on a day to day basis. There just felt as though there was never enough time in a day to accomplish the never-ending task. And as if my "to do list" was not long enough, there would be the continuous service request from my family, my friends, my church affiliates, my job and others.

Feeling stretched beyond measure, instead of attempting to gain a better understanding of WHY I was "called" I would silently (while anxiously overwhelmed) press through the day checking off my task list AND assisting others too.

As my walk with God deepened the parable "To whom much is given, much will be required" became vividly apparent to me. We are held responsible for what we have. We each are blessed with talents, gifts, resources, knowledge, time wealth and the like so, in turn it is expected that we give back. God wants us to use those gifts. We all need to ascertain the resources that God has abundantly showered on each one of us and fully use those resources that He has entrusted to us.

Early on in life it was apparent to me that I would be in the "helping" field. The more I furthered my education and my work experience, the more the demand became to continue to help others abundantly both personally and professionally. And with the understanding of this parable, it helped me to do what I was "called" to do with less anxiousness and more with ease.

What I know now is that:

- It is selfish to have God bless you with talents and gifts and not put them to use for the greater good
- Truly giving from the heart fills your life with joy and nourishes your soul
- "Giving" provides an intrinsic reward that's far more valuable than the gift
- Reciprocity builds positive and nurturing relationships
- The act of "giving" takes you out of yourself and allows you to expand beyond earthly limitations.
- When you are focused on giving to others, you are less likely to become consumed by your own concerns and challenges.

While it is true that we do not all have the same amount of money, we all do have time on our hands, and can give some of this time to coach, assist, promote, educate, nurture, empower and help others. Because if much has been given to you, much will be required of you. Accept and embrace it as you continue to live in HIS will for your life.

Twanda Grey

Your Inner Light

Isaiah 60:1

> Arise, shine; for thy light is come and the glory of the Lord is risen upon thee.

I attest and affirm...

I understand the power of recognizing your inner light. God gave each one of his children a special gift and skill set. Until you understand your potential, you his children haven't tapped into your purpose. The Holy Spirit of discernment allows us to tap into our light, through prayer, meditation, self-care and self-reflection. As women we must first take care of ourselves, before we can please others.

There has been a spiritual awakening going on in our lives. God calls his children to gain understanding of his will over your life. Our Father in Heaven has an assignment for each one of his children. Don't worry about your sister's light. Don't be distracted from your own blessings, by focusing on the blessings of others. God has also put that light in you queen, search and you shall find. As your find your inner light, you too will find your passion. Passion comes from the enjoyment of watching God use you in ways you never dreamed of. The feeling of living in your purpose is indescribable. When God calls his children, we must obediently answer!

Today I challenge you to tap into your talent. Ask yourself what you love to do in life. Whether it be taking photos, speaking at different events or beading necklaces; there's a need somewhere in this world to exercise your gift. There are places to go share your talent and make a living from your gift. God has given us one life! I don't believe our Father put us here to do for other's and neglect ourselves. This is our time to contribute and help the world see unity and peace by shining our lights together. Spreading our God given gifts amongst each other is self-fulfilling and empowering.

Ke'sha Dennis

Embrace Your Calling

Matthew 6:10

> Thy kingdom come, thy will be done in earth, as it is in Heaven.

I attest and affirm...

    I stopped running from what God called me to do and started embracing the calling. We all have gifts and talents that God has given us. Our gifts and talents are not meant to be bottled up and stored away here on earth. The will of God shall be done here on earth as it is already written in Heaven. Sometimes we allow our fear, and the opinions of others to diminish our dreams, aspirations and goals. God is our number one supporter, our number one cheerleader, and if he be for us, who can come against us. He wants to see us succeed and prosper for his Glory. He calls us safe, he calls us loved, and he calls us healed in every area of our life. God has given us direct access here on earth as it is already done in Heaven. We must speak those things that be not, as though they were. I speak a renewed mind, I speak a clean heart, I speak a renewed spirit, I speak life upon your dry bones. Wake up, mount your wings and take flight. For every breath you take you have been granted new mercies, and grace. Stop taking life for granted, stop wasting time having a pity party, we have been given the keys to Salvation. If we don't do anything else here on earth, at least give God a Hallelujah! He has been your Jehovah Jireh, Jehovah Nissi, Jehovah Rapha, and your Jehovah Shalom. We deny God our time, our talents, and our treasures repeatedly. Has he ever given up on us? Has he ever failed us? He has been the judge in a court case, he has been a comforter in the time of need, he has been a provider when there was no money, he has been your peace in the storm, he has been your light in the darkness, he has been the doctor in surgery, and he has been the strength of your life. I challenge you to be a vessel, go out and mentor, go out and encourage, go out a love, and most importantly go out and sow using your God giving gifts because he only see's the best in you.

Carol Terrell

Matthew 6:10

Thy kingdom come, Thy will be done in earth, as it is in Heaven.

I attest and affirm….

Shameless I am

Psalms 22:5

> They cried out to You and were delivered; They trusted in You and were not disappointed or ashamed.

I attest and affirm...

I am no longer ashamed. I'm not who I say I am, but I am who God says I am. I will no longer use my mouth to tear myself down, instead I will use my tongue to edify, encourage, and uplift. I'm not my past indiscretions, or shortcomings, and I'm not what I did, but I am the results of the lessons learned. I will not let my pastor or church folk shame me for not praying the way they think I should, or for missing a church service or two. I won't let my past stop me from believing I'm worthy of the greatest love; GOD's LOVE! I am no longer guilty of having a child by a married man, nor am I ashamed of keeping my child. I won't accept my daughter is anything less than a blessing, because God doesn't make mistakes. I will not allow anyone to condemn me for something I have already been forgiven for. I will not beat myself up for not obeying God when he first told me to move and go forward. I am not ashamed of who I was, and I am not ashamed of my failures. My failures helped to mold me into the rare gifted educated mompreneur (G.E.M.) I am today. I know the comeback is always greater than the setback and God has already spoken into my life. I am a force to be reckon with and therefore the devil tries his hardest to knock me down and keep me down. People tried to speak ill will over my life, but I don't receive it. I am no longer imprisoned by the word's others try to speak over me, because shame is a lie. Today I stand comfortable with who I am and no longer bound by negative thoughts, Amen!

Ayeisha Latta-Matthews

I Am Bold

Ephesians 3:12

> In whom we have boldness and access with confidence by the faith of him.

I attest and affirm...

I am bold. I just recently made a vision board saying I need to be bolder, less passive, more upfront, less prone to beat around the bush. God has given a purpose to you specifically. You must take ownership of the gifts you have been granted. You must be bold now in this moment. Overcome your insecurities and any need for reassurance.

I truly affirm that I will get to that point. God will help me get to that point. If it's you who struggles with this, please know that it is okay to be who you are. In God, you have all the assurance that you need. You do not have to dampen your light for anybody. If you don't agree with their approach or they differ from your approach, it doesn't matter. If you are going to live in your truth, you must be bold. You are going to be glad that God gave you what he gave you. Your gifts set you apart and make you unique.

I continue working on this. If you are like me, know that you are not alone. God gave me something he didn't give anybody else. I should not be ashamed. I must be strategic in my wording and careful in my actions. I must move with the spirit of Christ. But I'm not going to be scared anymore. I'm not going to be bashful. I am going to be who God called me to be. I, Jade Cross-French, attest and affirm that I am bold in Christ.

Jade Cross-French

God Answers

Matthew 7:7

> Ask and it will be given to you, seek and you will find; knock and it will be opened to you.

I attest and affirm...

I have asked God to grant me my dreams. I believed I was ready to receive them only to learn that receiving what you want doesn't always have a happy ending. We've all heard our grandmothers say, "Be careful what you pray for!" Well, let's just say that I had to learn this the hard way.

Unfortunately, there's many times in life where we forgot to let God take the wheel. If God allowed Satan to test his son, who are we to question his will? I remember a time where I was angry at God for doing his job of saving me from myself! I asked God to remove those who aren't beneficial to my life and he showed out. I lost so called family members, friends and associates. We begin to learn that God calls his children in his timing. When he wants us alone for us to clearly hear him; he will remove everyone from around us to get our attention. When we're still, long enough to hear that sound or feel that feeling we are tuning into Gods will over our lives. Some call it intuition. I like to call it interstitial kinesthetics, because it's an energy source that radiates throughout every part of your body. The answer is right there in front of us and many times we miss Gods will for our lives, because we don't like the vision or answer we receive.

As I continue my journey through life, I've made it my mission to let go and let God. Everybody isn't for everybody and just because it sounds or looks good, doesn't mean it's good for you. The older I become the more respect I have for the women who've walked the path before me. There were times I thought my mom was being weak, only to realize that's where her strength lied. I remember times thinking my aunt was being mean only to realize now, she was coming from a place of love. I thank God for every lesson and blessing, because they've shaped me into the woman I am today. I ask that we as women will continue to share the stories that have molded us into the queens we have become.

We all need to continue to share our stories as strength for those going through what we've been through. Our testimonies are for the motherless child, the broken homegirl, the rich outcast, the weird ones at school, the smart ones, the insecure girl and the ones who are simply different. I can relate to you all. God bless everyone reading this book, God's will on your life is already planned. Go be great at any and everything you do!

Ke'sha Dennis

Despair is Temporary

Psalm 34:17-20

> When the righteous cry for help, the Lord hears and delivers them out of all their troubles. The Lord is near to the brokenhearted and saves the crushed in spirit. Many are the afflictions of the righteous, but the Lord delivers him out of them all. He keeps all his bones; not one of them is broken.

1 Peter 5:7

> God has mended my mind, heart and spirit for this day onward I will cast all my anxieties to God.

I attest and affirm...

I too, once felt shattered and broken, lost until I found my way back home. Home, where I communicate with God and turn over all my worries and woes over to him. How many Beloveds have felt this way, lost and alone? My Beloved, I have come to let you know there are many. You are not alone in your feelings of despair, for they are what makes us all human. As we share our feelings of joy, so too must we share our feelings of despair in order to heal. Do not Beloved let your hurts and pains bind you into darkness.

Let your light be the beacon of love, trust and friendship. Be your true self. For you were not created by mistake, you were created by need and love. You, my Beloved are a living Angel, with God given gifts that are desperately needed.

Come take your place among your brethren and allow us to help you heal. Rise with a smile knowing, you may feel shattered, however, you are not broken. Take your place among the masses, knowing you were ordained at birth to be a part of something greater than man could ever imagine. Sow a seed of faith, in yourself and humanity. Come now, Beloved you are wanted and need!

Maureen Brewster

1 Peter 5:7

God has mended my mind, heart and spirit for this day onward I will cast all my anxieties to God.

I attest and affirm….

Live in the Present

Matthew 6:34

> So do not worry about tomorrow; for tomorrow will worry about itself. Each day has enough trouble of its own.

I attest and affirm...

I will live in the present moment and enjoy life. Given the fast pace and hectic schedules most of us keep, a base level of anxiety, stress, and unhappiness is the new norm. You may not even realize it, but this tendency to get sucked into the past and the future can leave you perpetually worn out and feeling out of touch with yourself.

The past is remembered, and the future is hoped for, but many of us live most of our lives reflecting backwards. Living in the now is so difficult because we are always encouraged to think about the future or dwell on our past. How many times have you been in the middle of one thing and suddenly began re-channeling your mind and energy to something else? I am sure we can all relate to this. Spending energy on time we can never get back!

It is good to think about the past and future sometimes. Where would we be if we didn't look back over our past successes and mistakes and learn from them? Where would we be if we never planned for the future or prepared ourselves for what is to come? But creating a balance of how often your inter-changeably reflect on the past and/or daydream about the future is vital.

Being in the present moment, or the "here and now," means that we are aware and mindful of what is happening at this very moment. We are not distracted by ruminations on the past or worries about the future but centered in the here and now. All of our attention is focused on the present moment

Consciously assess how often you spent too much time reflecting on the past or focusing on the future. The more you are aware, the more control you will have in practicing mindfulness techniques to stay in the present moment. Try deep breathing; or Yoga; Take a walk; any mindfulness techniques that require you to be attentive to the here and now.

Living life is not meant to simply exist, but to enjoy being alive presently…. Choose to enjoy the simple pleasantries of life and practice living in the current moment! After all, once time passes, we can never get it back.

Twanda Grey

I Am Better

Psalms 60:12

Through God we will have victory, For He will trample down our enemies.

I attest and affirm...

I am no longer bitter. Though I have been hurt by loved ones, lied on by friends, cheated on and disrespected by lovers, I am no longer in a state of anger. I will no longer give power to those who tried to disrupt my spirit. Today I am taking the "I" out of Bitter and replacing it with an "E". I will take all of life's lessons and use them to become a better person. I am not lost instead I've found peace in knowing God will fight my battles. I know better and I will continue to do better. The actions of others will not cause me to sin and lose sight of what is most important. I am not my old vengeful, and angry self, but Lord if any of the old feelings try to rise, I ask for you to help me let go of any animosity, resentment, and rage. I have killed the weeds that were strangling my roots. Those feelings have no place in my heart, please awaken the Holy Spirit in my heart so I can continue to move in Love. I need to remain in your will, so please help me to pray for those who prey on me and my family. Satan is aware of the promises on my life and I will not take the bait and bow down to his tricks. If you find anything in me that is not of you, I surrender those toxic emotions, and I ask you for your forgiveness. Once I figured out, I have the power to do any and everything I put my mind if it is according to Gods word, I became unstoppable. Lord thank you for your son Jesus it because of him, Today I stand VICTORIOUS!

Ayeisha Latta-Matthews

I Will Break Generational Curses

Joel 1:3

> Tell it to your children, and let your children tell it to their children, and their children to the next generation.

I attest and affirm...

I will break generational curses. Times are drastically changing. I want my children to know that they have options. They can choose the life that they live. They can build from a firm foundation and live life to the fullest. Or, they can live as a hostage to the life they started off with which wasn't that great.

I am learning better ways to teach my kids the things that they need to know. This scripture goes deeper than the surface. If we don't teach our kids, who's going to teach them. No one else is going to teach them. We must tell them the secrets so they can tell their children. Their children will tell their children and their children's children. They will live a different, more prosperous, and better-informed existence when they become our age. They will be proud and satisfied when they see who they are becoming.

I love this because I'm consistently involved at my kids' school. My son just started preschool at a public school. He doesn't sit still. I felt like wasn't reflecting the parenting he received at home. It made me sad, but then I think about God. He has control of it all. He's going to make it work. I stay in my word. I stay as quiet as I can possibly be, but I watch my kids. I'll make sure that they talk so that they can teach. Today I attest and affirm that I will break this generational curse.

Jade Cross-French

The Gift of Praise

1 Thessalonians 5: 16-18

> Rejoice evermore. Pray without ceasing. In everything give thanks: For this is the will of God in Christ Jesus concerning you.

I attest and affirm...

Every day God allows me to wake up with breath in my body, the activity of my limbs, and clothed in my right mind I will thank him. We tend to take life for granted. We look at where we are right now, and what's not right in your life. We start complaining and turning into the accuser of the brethren. We blame it on our upbringing and generational curses. We look at our friends or other people and start comparing what they have opposed to what we have. We start to idolize their cars, their homes, their clothes, and their lifestyle and then want to be like them. In addition, we start questioning God about why they are blessed when they do not go to church, they do not sow into others, they are mean and selfish. We need to start holding ourselves accountable for where we are in life. We get complacent, and comfortable in bad situations and do absolutely nothing to change it. We sit and soak in sorrow and then find ourselves holding everyone else accountable for disappointments. We only pray when things are not right in our lives, we only dance like David when things are great in our lives but I decree and declare from this day forward you will rejoice evermore for every breath that you take, for the roof over your head, for the food you are able to eat, and for the $9.00 an hour that you make on your job. Just remember when we are complaining about where we are in life and what we have, you better be careful about coveting thy neighbor's goods. The devil is in the business of blessing. Appreciate where you are in life because God knew your end before your beginning. Delayed does not mean denied! The last shall finish first but be not weary in well doing. Always remember that if you think your situation is bad, there is someone else worse off than you, and guess what they are rejoicing evermore, they are praying without ceasing, they are dancing like David, and they are thanking God as if they were you. They are praising and glorifying God for the very blessings that you already have and are complaining about.

    Carol Terrell

1 Thessalonians 5: 16-18

> Rejoice evermore. Pray without ceasing. In everything give thanks: For this is the will of God in Christ Jesus concerning you.

I attest and affirm....

_____
_____
_____
_____
_____
_____
_____
_____
_____
_____
_____
_____
_____
_____
_____
_____
_____
_____
_____
_____
_____
_____

Loving God

Deuteronomy 6:4-6

> Hear, O Israel: The Lord our God, the Lord is one. Love the Lord your God with all your heart and with all your soul and with all your strength. These commandments that I give you today are to be on your hearts.

I attest and affirm...

Loving God means we must seek him all day every day. As we gracefully age each day seems to fly by. Sometimes we get caught up in our daily routines and we forget to thank the one that made the day possible. God calls the children of Israel to love him with all our hearts. We are not obeying God when we don't put our trust in him.

This may be a daily struggle, because we tend to have the need to be in control. The moment you think you're in control, you'll soon find out how out of control things are. Although I know this scripture is true, I have found myself struggling to get out of my own way at times. These are the times I remove myself from others and listen to what God is showing me. I do this by stepping outside of myself and looking back in. Everyone has their own version of you. Step outside of yourself, to see how the world envisions you.

Take the time to take that drive and call on God. When the kids fall asleep and you're getting ready for bed, thank him for your life. When you're at the hospital waiting on those test results, say a prayer. These are our moments; God has set aside for us to reach out to him.

I thank God for the small things in life. Things I've taken for granted. God saw something special in me, before I saw it in myself and for that, I try to thank him as often as I can. I fall short many days, but I continue to be the best version of me I can. We must all do our best.

Ke'sha   Dennis

It Wasn't My Fault

Romans 12:2

> Do not be conformed to this world, but be transformed by the renewing of your mind, that you may prove what is that good and acceptable and perfect will of God.

I attest and affirm...

I will no longer hold myself responsible for the action of another. I will no longer accuse myself of not being able to fight or fend off my attacker. I will no longer tell myself I could have prevented what happened to me. There was nothing I could have done differently to prevent what happened that dreadful day. I will not let what society says affect what I believe about myself. The face I portray to the world will be a face of pride, boldness, fulfillment, and authenticity. I know what happened to me I couldn't have stopped, so Lord please stop the broken record from playing repeatedly in my mind. I still was upset at myself and I gave every reason why I should have been able to escape. How I should have been able to break free.

My mind takes me back to the very space in time and I felt so weak. I know that I am not a weak person, I am a strong person. Though I was taken advantage of, today I take back my power that I allowed my perpetrator to have. I am no longer wearing the mask of hate instead I make a conscience effort to love. I will only analyze the facts and not the what ifs. I can't change what happened to me, but I can change how I allow it to affect every aspect of my life. I'm taking back my peace of mind, and I'm not just happy, but I've got my joy back. Today I find no fault of mine in what I was a victim to. I am no longer a Prisoner to fear, pain, hurt, anger, and guilt, Today I take back my life, I have been set free!

Ayeisha Latta-Matthews

Start Trusting

Matthew 6:25

> Therefore, I tell you, stop being worried or anxious about your life, as to what you will eat or what you will drink; nor about your body as to what you will wear.

I attest and affirm...

I will stop worrying and start trusting. If only the infamous song "Don't worry be happy" could be the solution for worry! Any time we are tempted to be worried or anxious, we can find help and encouragement in Matthew 6:25. The definition of worry is

> :to give way to anxiety or unease; allow one's mind to dwell on difficulty or troubles.

Gods instructions are clear for us to stop being anxious and worried especially concerning provisions for our everyday needs. At times this may be easier said than done, however, when we continuously bombard ourselves with negative thoughts and feelings with worry and anxious thoughts, we are disobeying one of Gods commands.

It is common to have unpleasant thoughts that at times cause worry. But what you do with that thought is what is important. You can exercise control over your thoughts. You can choose to worry, or you can reject worry and choose to live with joy and peace.

Truth of the matter is that worrying is within your control. When we worry, we are indicating that we doubt that God will take care of us or meet our needs. You have authority over those thoughts! Put them in Captivity!

Command those automatic thoughts! My favorite saying is "NOT TA DAY!" when worry attempts to captivate my thoughts, disturb my peace and cause me to doubt and disobey my Creator.

Daily I ask God to help me not to worry about anything and to trust HIM in everything because I am confident that HE will take care of me. God "I Trust YOU!"

This verse and its teachings indicate that we are not to worry about anything in life. This is not to say that we should never think and plan, however it indicates that we should not be fearful and filled with worry while doing so. When we worry and are fearful, we forfeit our peace.

Work on disciplining your mind. Taking your thoughts captive simply means gaining control over what you think about yourself and life. Know that we can find hope, peace and confidence in the fact that God knows exactly what we need and promises to provide for us.

Twanda Grey

I Speak Wealth, Abundance and Life

Proverbs 23:16

Yea, my reins shall rejoice, when thy lips speak right things.

I attest and affirm...

I speak wealth, abundance, and life. I often find myself speaking negatively and complaining because things aren't going my way. Later more negative things start to happen because of the things that I say out my mouth. You don't want to be that person that nobody wants to talk to because you're always talking negative. This is something I found myself doing. It was my pattern and that of some of my friends. I have worked on it. I now speak more positively about my life, my aspirations, and my challenges. Words really create reality. Words link to your thoughts.

I'm going to share a mind trick. Think of something that God would tell you to do or what He would want you to say to glorify him. Instead of complaining about what's going on, focus on everything beautiful and God's handiwork. Everything he does is for the good. I'm going to start trusting in what God says. I will begin to express gratitude towards things I'm grateful for.

Jade Cross-French

Proverbs 23:16

Yea, my reins shall rejoice, when thy lips speak right things.

I attest and affirm….

_____
_____
_____
_____
_____
_____
_____
_____
_____
_____
_____
_____
_____
_____
_____
_____
_____
_____
_____
_____

Speak Wisely

Matthew 12:36-37

> But I tell you that everyone will have to give account on the day of judgement for every empty word they have spoken. For by your words you will be acquitted, and by your words you will be condemned.

I attest and affirm...

I must speak wisely. We are held accountable by God for every word that comes from our mouths. Everyone who knew the old version of me, would tell you that I used to curse like a sailor. I'm not sure why I spoke foul language, but I'd been talking that way for years, until I realized how inappropriate it sounded. Not only were my daughters watching, God was watching the entire time. As I came across this scripture, I felt shame on me for not understanding the power of bad words. Everyone has their own revelations at different times of their lives. I had mine in my late thirties.

I sometimes find myself going backwards and I must remind myself that it's not okay to use harsh words. Although I rarely, if ever curse; I do use mean choice words at time. Whether it's when I'm irritated that the person in front of me that didn't signal before jumping into my lane, or I'm yelling at my children for not doing what I asked of them; I must remember Gods words. We must take accountability for every word that comes out of our mouths. Today I remain in prayer that I use my words wisely. Being of flesh we will sin and fall short at times, but we must go to God for help during these times. We must also apologize to those we've hurt using harsh words.

Ke'sha Dennis

Speak Life

Psalm 141:3

> Set a guard over my mouth, LORD; keep watch over the door of my lips.

I attest and affirm...

I will speak words to uplift and empower.

'In the beginning was the Word, and the Word was with God, and the Word was God."

We could all learn something from this well-known Bible verse. There is a message to be found in this for everyone. Everything begins with a word. God tells us in His Word that the tongue has incredible power. We can use our tongue to bring blessings and life or curses and death. That childhood chant "sticks and stones can break my bones, but words will never hurt me" is simply not true. Our tongues can be the most difficult thing to control and leave us with great regret.

Words have energy and power with the ability to help, to heal, to hinder, to hurt, to harm, to humiliate and to humble. There is a time to speak and a time to keep silent. Sometimes the best thing we can do is to say nothing. When we do speak, it is wise to be purposeful in what we say to ourselves and to others; and to think about our words beforehand. The more we understand the power of our words, the more we will want to grow in speaking positively and using our words for good.

Begin to speak positively over your life for starters. Choose the words that you speak consciously. Practice improved self-awareness over the words that you use to describe yourself and your life. Negative, powerless words such as "can't', shouldn't', 'need', 'won't' should all be avoided. They strip you of your ability to manifest a life that you want to live.

Be kind to all others and speak words that are beacons of inspiration, enthusiasm and encouragement to the people you encounter. When we speak, we should speak with mindfulness, in a way to solidify peace and compassion in our characters.

Your words create the story with which becomes your reality. When we put those negative words out there, they become our reality. Choose your words wisely and positively and speak always remember to speak life!

Twanda Grey

Choose Your Words Wisely

Proverbs 15:4

> Gentle words bring life and health; a deceitful tongue crushes the spirit

I attest and affirm...

I will choose my words wisely. Words. We can choose to use them to encourage, or destructively use them to cause despair. Words have energy and power with the ability to help, to heal, to hinder, to hurt, to harm, to humiliate and to humble.

For example: Think about the words to a favorite spiritual song. How do you feel afterwards? Or think on a time when you may have encountered a person who may have offer a kind word. Reflect how it immediately awakened the senses and may have boosted your endorphins. Leaving you with feelings of happiness, hope, inspiration, motivation and encouragement. Words have power!

It is important that we discipline ourselves to speak in a way that puts that positive energy with hopes of reciprocity. It conveys respect, gentleness and humility. Many times, it is not what you need to say, but how you say it. Take the time to pause before making comments or responding to be sure that there is room for ill intent in what you want to convey.

Be mindful to do a self-check regarding your emotional well-being when communicating with others. Aim to communicate with empathy and understanding despite your opinion about the matter. There are certain rules that should guide all our communications when dialoguing with others. Aim to speak the truth and avoid exaggeration. Be consistent in what you are saying. Stay away from using double standards in addressing people. Refrain from using words to manipulate others, and most importantly do not use words to insult or belittle anyone.

Learn to listen patiently and speak tactfully as you tell the truth of how you understand the content of the message. I will say it again... Words hold great power. Words are the symbols of life, of language, of all that we know and feel. Words give expression to our lives, our souls, our deepest longings and strongest emotions. And the skill of using the right words is a potent force.

Never, ever, *ever* underestimate the power your words can have. The power is in the tongue.

Twanda Grey

Yes HE Can

Philippians 4:13

I can do all things through Christ who strengthens me.

I attest and affirm...

I will no longer say I can't. From this day forward I will say I can because HE can, and he will. I will finish what I started a day ago, a week ago, a month ago, and a year ago because I can do any and everything, I put my mind to with the help of the Lord. I will no longer live in fear or in doubt. I know my future is better than my current situation, and though I don't know what the future holds I will walk by faith and not by sight. I will no longer exempt myself from receiving what I have asked for according to the word of God. I will continue to go through and trust the process even when I am faced with trials and tribulations. I know God is a way maker and situation shifter. God heard all my prayers since I was a child and he has answered everyone one of them. I know he doesn't always say yes or even give me what I ask for right now, but he is an on-time God. Many weapons will be formed against me, but I stand firm on his word that they will not prosper. There is absolutely nothing this world can give me that God hasn't already provided me. The God I serve is a great God, and MY God can and will move mountains. Lord help me to exercise my faith, and do my part, because faith without works is dead. I often ask God what he can do for me and tell him what I need but starting today I will ask God what I can do for him. Lord how can I serve you? How can I bring Glory unto you?

Ayeisha Latta-Matthews

Philippians 4:13

I can do all things through Christ who strengthens me.

I attest and affirm....

I Am Secure

Psalms 30:6

When I felt secure, I said, "I will never be shaken."

I attest and affirm...

I am secure. Whew, this scripture just speaks to me. Allow me to share the journey I took. I listened to the opinions of others. Everyone told me what to do. I never did what I wanted to do because I felt like I didn't really have what it took. In that, I wasted so much time. I was broke. I was sad. I had babies depending on me. I had a man that leaned on me.

The beginning of my entrepreneurship journey witnessed my lights being turned off due to nonpayment. It was the most embarrassing event that ever happened to me. I was so ashamed. My kids were two and three years old. They didn't know what was going on. Nobody in my family but my grandmother who raised me knew.

One day my son said, "I want to go home and get naked."

"You are only three years old. What you know about that?" I scolded jokingly. But in my heart and mind I felt like such a failure. At that moment, I knew it would never never never in my life happen again. How dare I let my own dreams put my family in such a predicament. I kept my lights on by any legal means necessary.

God always has my back. But I learned the lesson of security. The desire to stay clear of that situation motivates me to rise every morning and put in the work. I will never be shaken. I will never go back. I will never take the easy way to laziness. I am committed and self-motivated. I am secure in Jesus name. Amen.

Jade Cross-French

Suicide Loses

Psalms 34:18

The Lord is near to the heartbroken and he saves those who are crushed in spirit (contrite in heart, truly sorry for their sin).

I attest and affirm...

God has control over my life. The devil has no reign over my life, and he is not in control of my thoughts. I will no longer hide behind the urge to end it all. I have thoughts of how to take my life, but today I chose to live. I know this is not the end of my journey, and my story is not over. I have so much to offer this world. I have so much to learn and so much to give. I am not my pain, my hurt, hopelessness, sadness, nor do I hate myself. Lord please forgive me for no longer wanting to live and wishing I was dead. I was mad I was still alive when I woke up today, and I am sad because today is my daughter's birthday. Forgive me for being so selfish and closed minded. Forgive me for not considering her feelings and the devastation she would endure if I were to leave this world right now. Lord, I feel as though the world doesn't deserve to have me in it but thank you Lord for reminding me, I'm here to be a servant to your people. Forgive me for not appreciating even the smallest of things. Forgive me for hating my life though I am blessed beyond measure. Today I've found hope, I've regained my strength to want to continue this thing we call LIFE. I love myself unconditionally and I need to be here, because the world needs more like me. On everyday going forward, the devil will lose. He has no place this day and all the days to come. He will take not rest in my mind or in my heart. There is light at the end of the tunnel and my glass is half full. **I WIN!!**

Ayeisha Latta-Matthews

I Have Friends That Understand

Proverbs 17:17

A friend loves at all times, and a brother is born for adversity.

I attest and affirm...

I have friends that understand. Even though my friends don't always agree with me and vice versa, we are always there to love one another to encourage one another. I really like the words of this verse because a brother is born for adversity. That means when you struggle, your friend is supposed to have your back. When you fall, they help you get back up. They're supposed to talk about today not make you feel shame for your past. They make you feel hopeful not like you're less than what you are. They are always supposed to be honest with give constructive criticism and not have you out here looking like you are crazy. They should provide you that unconditional love that exemplifies a friend's commitment.

I love the circle that God has brought around me. Even though I don't talk to them every day, I know that I can give them a call. Most of my friends are older than me, but they're present when I need them. Each friend has different skills and capacities. Be careful what you tell and who you tell. Some people can help in some situations and are harmful in others. They don't mean you bad. It's just not their area of expertise. Keep your eye on the prize. God will put people in your life that you can lean on when you are having a tough time.

    Jade   Cross-French

I Am Alive

1 Peter 2:9

> But you are a chosen people, a royal priesthood, a holy nation, God's special possession, that you may declare the praises of him who you out of darkness into his wonderful light.

I attest and affirm...

I am alive. On days when I feel like giving up I will P.U.S.H. When I no longer want to go on, I will remember what I am going through is just a test, so one day I will be able to share my testimony. I am alive to give back, to pour life into the lifeless, and to help those who are lost and can't seem to find their way. I am alive not by chance but on purpose. I have been going through a drought, but I'm learning to re-love my life, re-love who I am where I am right now. When I was feeling great, my career was good, and I was comfortable it was easy to have faith and believe that all things are possible if I keep my mind stayed on Jesus. I have been through so much and have made a mess out of many situations. I will allow my many messes have become my message, and I vow to help someone who is going through what I went through. Help to be content and unconflicted in my mind, body and soul. I pray my reward in heaven will be greater than I can possibly imagine. No matter what the devil did is doing, I will stand firm in the Word of God. My faith will be tested, but my faith in Jesus will not falter. No matter how spiteful people are, and no matter the attacks on my character, I will stay upright and remain strong. I will continue to fight the good fight in this world can be and no matter the attacks that are being done to my wellbeing, I will always proclaim that Jesus is a healer a deliverer and God is now and forever more! **MY story is not finished!**

Ayeisha Latta-Matthews

I Will Guard My Surroundings

Proverbs 22:10

>Drive out the mocker, and out goes strife; quarrels and insults are ended.

I attest and affirm...

I will guard my surroundings. I will practice discernment and choose wisely those who I entertain.

Have you ever hit a point in life where you would just completely surrounded by drama? You feel like there was no way out. Or, you feel a super big issue going on. You try in vain to figure out your place in all the drama.

Sometimes, the problem is not you. You must separate from people sometimes. No matter how much you like them, no matter how much money they have, no matter how many connections they have, they are simply just a drama-prone person. Nothing to do about it.

I have had my share of these experiences. I have had to separate from people that I really like. I don't like having issues with people, but sometimes those people bring the issues.

We must all strive to discern what people are truly about. Pay attention to their conversation. If the good outweighs the bad that's a start. If the bad is not detrimental deal breakers, that's a win. Don't drop anybody just because I wrote this point in this book. Pay attention to how much attention they pay to negativity instead of what God has given them. Notice whether they express gratitude for the things that they do have.

Jade Cross-French

Proverbs 22:10

Drive out the mocker, and out goes strife; quarrels and insults are ended.

I attest and affirm….

Through the Eyes of Depression

Isaiah 60:1

> Arise (from spiritual depression to a new life), shine (be radiant with the glory and brilliance of the Lord); for your light has come, And the glory and brilliance of the Lord has risen upon you.

I attest and affirm...

I am not depression. I will no longer avoid washing the dishes or doing the laundry for weeks at a time. When I feel broken, sad, hurt, deep regret, or conflicted, I will remind myself that I am an overcomer. I will no longer stay in the bed all day because I am afraid to face the world. I will stay committed to the things I agreed to do, and I will keep my word. I won't make up excuses to avoid being around others. I will get out of the bed, brush my teeth and wash my face daily no matter how I feel. I will leave the house at least three times a week and smile at one person. I will no longer hate myself because I know I am not being a great mom, wife or friend. I will ask for help when I need it and recognize that asking for help doesn't mean I'm not independent. I will no longer binge eat because that is the only thing that will comfort me. I am not afraid to be in my house by myself and just because I am alone doesn't make me lonely. There are times I feel

I cannot cope, help me find peace by reassuring me you are here. I am not a failure and I believe all things are possible with God. There will be times when I am sad, but I will fight to avoid becoming depressed. I know depression is not just about being sad. It can be debilitating, cause guilt, hopelessness, shame, numbness, exhaustion, lack of motivation, and emptiness. I will not let my anxiety take complete control over my life. I am no longer a prisoner in my mind, and the shackles have been removed. Today I am renewed, Hallelujah!

Ayeisha Latta-Matthews

I Will Not Argue

Proverbs 25:9

> If you argue your case with a neighbor, do not betray another man's confidence.

I attest and affirm...

I will not argue. Trying to prove my point is pointless. Don't talk down to anybody if they don't agree on something that you believed to be true. I don't want anybody to feel less than. That is truly one of my goals. Don't tear anybody down because you feel that you are right, and they are wrong. Everybody is entitled to their opinion. Everyone is also their own person. There's no sense in making enemies. If someone doesn't agree with you, that is fine. The unity that we need to possess goes far beyond disagreement on any one issue.

Use a discerning spirit when you are dealing with situations like this because you might be up against the fight that you are unaware of. Sometimes we get in our feelings and feel like we must prove we are right. When somebody may be trying to instruct you or give you advice, listen. Even though you may not agree, it's not purposeful to argue your point. You cannot learn without listening.

Stay positive and believe. If anything, ever makes you unsure, pray and listen for the guidance that's going to be provided for you afterward. It is always there. The inner voice that tells you the right thing to do, that is God.

I haven't had too many run-ins with this, but when I do encounter this, I just sit back and observe. I'll continue to test the spirits in my environment. I am careful not to welcome negative spirits in. Knowing that I don't have all the answers is no worry. I know God does. I choose to believe in him. I don't argue with people because people aren't my God.

Jade Cross-French

I Trust You

Proverbs 3:5

Trust in the Lord with all your heart and lean not on your own understanding.

I attest and affirm...

I trust you with every fiber in my body. I will trust in the Lord when I am in my darkest hour. When the rent is due and I have no source of income, I trust you Lord. Even when I can't see or understand why I am hurting I will trust in your ability to get me through. Though cancer took my brother, and I couldn't understand why at such a young age, I will trust you. I will trust you though my child has cancer and I will trust in you even though my grandmother was called home unexpectedly. When I can't see a way out of my current circumstances, I know your plans for my life exceed them. I will keep my faith in you when all odds are against me. I will believe in you when my life is a living hell. I trust every promise you said was mine I will receive. When I am in trouble, I will look to you to deliver me from my enemies. When I am scared, I will cast my cares to you. I can't continue to worry about things I don't have the power to change, so Lord help me to be okay with the outcome. With all the craziness going on in the world, I am desperate for you. he world is in desperate need of your presence and I need you like never. I trust that when my mind is racing you will silence the voices that tell me I can't. I trust that you will mend my broken heart and allow me to love unconditionally and receive love without thinking there is a hidden agenda. I trust that you will send me my soul mate and I will be cherished. My trust in you is limitless!

Ayeisha Latta-Matthews

Proverbs 3:5

Trust in the Lord with all your heart and lean not on your own understanding.

I attest and affirm....

I Will Wait on the Lord

Psalms 27:14

> Wait on the LORD: be of good courage, and he shall strengthen thine heart: wait, I say, on the LORD.

I attest and affirm...

I will wait on the Lord. This is a crucial piece of anything that you do. Sometimes, I jump ahead of myself and do things out of order. When it turns out bad, I look sad or disappointed. It is not what God wanted for me. I was hardheaded, so I got whooped for it. When I find myself thinking that I know better than God, it gets me confused. Confusion opens me up for enemies to attack me. Things are stolen from me. A lot of different things start happening that are not good.

I now pray before I do anything. I pray before I go to work. I pray before I go and solidify a business partnership. I even prayed before I dived into my portion of this book. I really want what I do to be as Divine as possible. I know that I'm not perfect. But God knows what is best for me. He is not going to leave me anywhere that is going to harm me. Even if it gets super challenging, I know that guy always has my back no matter what. I choose to trust him. If I don't know, I wait for him to answer or I use my discernment to fill out whether this is something that God really wants me to do or not.

    Jade   Cross-French

I Receive My Healing

Proverbs 4:22

> For they are life to those who find them, And healing and health to all their flesh.

I attest and affirm...

    I am healed. I come in the name of Jesus, thanking him for his divine power. Lord please forgive us for any sins we may have committed knowingly and unknowingly. I pray I remain encouraged and believe there is Power in the name of Jesus, healing in the name of Jesus, deliverance in the name of Jesus, and strength to continue the good fight in the name of Jesus. Lord I pray you cleanse and purify not just my body, but my mind as well. I give to you the memories that haunt me day and night. I rebuke rheumatoid arthritis, migraine headaches, back spasms, plantar fasciitis and any other ailments that have taken shelter in my body in the name of Jesus. I speak life and healing over every inch of my body. From the top of my head to the soles of my feet. In the word of God, it says by his (Jesus) stripes we are healed, so it's a done deal and I am claiming wholeness right now, nothing broken, nothing missing, and nothing lacking. My heart has been broken many times than I can count, and Lord I ask for you to heal my heart. I want to love without boundaries and feel good about it. Help me to find peace as you walk alongside me as I walk throughout this world filled with so much discord. Heal my spiritual eyes and help me view people the way you do. Lord sustain me by your grace and heal me according to you will. Every cell in my body has been renewed, and I will begin to regain my strength and I will to rise greater than what I was yesterday. Satan's defeated, and I have the victory, in Jesus Name I pray Amen!

Ayeisha Latta-Matthews

Proverbs 4:22

For they are life to those who find them, And healing and health to all their flesh.

I attest and affirm….

I Will Listen to the Lord

Psalms 34 :11

> Come, my children, listen to me; I will teach you the fear of the LORD.

I attest and affirm...

I will listen to the Lord. After writing this, I know how to examine myself and examine how I have listened in the past. I can explore what it means to listen to the Lord. Sometimes he speaks to us in ways that we don't really understand. For me, it's a journey of trust. I really want to be in His grace. I don't want to do anything that makes Jesus upset.

Knowing that God wants us to prosper, I had to be okay with accepting some of the blessings that I really didn't understand. Through everything that I do, I pray. I pray that everything that I do is pleasing to the kingdom. That's my end goal. That's what I strive for.

Through everything, he teaches us how to deal with people. He teaches us how to be better entrepreneurs. He teaches us how to be better parents. He teaches us how to speak up for ourselves. He teaches us how to be everything that we want to be and more. Learning more about God, learning more about the word, and learning to decipher blessings is a choice to listen. I am still learning. I am making the choice, daily, to listen.

Jade Cross-French

Aim for a Forgiving Heart

Ephesians 4: 31-32

> Get rid of all bitterness, rage and anger, brawling and slander, along with every form of malice. Be kind and compassionate to one another, forgiving each other, just as in Christ God forgave you

I attest and affirm...

I will always aim to have a forgiving heart. Forgiveness is a conscious and deliberate decision to release feelings of resentment or vengeance toward someone who has harmed you. Forgiveness transforms anger and hurt into healing and peace. Forgiveness can help you overcome feelings of depression, anxiety, and rage, as well as personal and relational conflicts. It is about making the conscious decision to let go of a grudge.

Forgiveness is not so much for the other person, but it is for YOU! And that goes for forgiving yourself too. It is about setting yourself free so that you can move forward in your own life. It is not about pretending that what has happened is okay or re-establishing any form of relationship with a person.

The problem for many of us is that sometimes we can choose to forgive another, but still in our heart of hearts, the anger or resentment lingers. However, it is in fact possible to forgive and truly let go of past disappointments, hurts, or blatant acts of abuse. Although at times this may seem implausible, forgiveness is a teachable and learnable skill that can dramatically improve with practice over time.

Bitterness is mental prison. Forgiving a person who has wronged you is never easy but dwelling on those events and reliving them over and over can fill your mind with negative thoughts and suppressed anger. We can take all this pain, all this anger, and all these constant negative thoughts patterns and transform them into our personal opportunity to excel!

Allow the opportunity to encourage you to grow in character and leadership to aim at being a better person. Focus on letting the resentment go. Commit to forgiving yourself for your role and others for wrongdoing. When the memory of the wrongdoing reappears, give it a moment and then cast the thought down. Dwelling on it will only resurface the emotional pain. After all, the offense/act has already occurred; it's in the past; willingly forgive whether there will be a continued relationship or not. Free yourself emotionally. It is so vital to be able to move forward.

Twanda Grey

Ephesians 4: 31-32

Get rid of all bitterness, rage and anger, brawling and slander, along with every form of malice. Be kind and compassionate to one another, forgiving each other, just as in Christ God forgave you

I attest and affirm….

www.ingramcontent.com/pod-product-compliance
Lightning Source LLC
Chambersburg PA
CBHW032044150426
43194CB00006B/420